HOW TO GROW
FRUITS, VEGETABLES
& HOUSEPLANTS
WITHOUT SOIL

The Secrets of
Hydroponic Gardening Revealed

Rick Helweg

HOW TO GROW FRUITS, VEGETABLES & HOUSEPLANTS WITHOUT SOIL: THE SECRETS OF HYDROPONIC GARDENING REVEALED

Library of Congress Cataloging-in-Publication Data

Helweg, Richard, 1956-

How to grow fruits, vegetables & houseplants without soil : the secrets of hydroponic gardening revealed / by Rick Helweg.
pages cm
Other title: Secrets of hydroponic gardening revealed
Includes bibliographical references and index.

ISBN 978-1-60138-600-7 (alk. paper) -- ISBN 1-60138-600-1 (alk. paper) 1. Hydroponics. I. Title. II. Title: Secrets of hydroponic gardening revealed.

SB126.5.H45 2014
631.5'85--dc23
2013045471

Printed in the United States

Printed on Recycled Paper

INTERIOR LAYOUT: Antoinette D'Amore • addesign@videotron.ca
COVER DESIGN: Meg Buchner • megadesn@mchsi.com

A few years back we lost our beloved pet dog Bear, who was not only our best and dearest friend but also the "Vice President of Sunshine" here at Atlantic Publishing. He did not receive a salary but worked tirelessly 24 hours a day to please his parents.

Bear was a rescue dog who turned around and showered myself, my wife, Sherri, his grandparents Jean, Bob, and Nancy, and every person and animal he met (well, maybe not rabbits) with friendship and love. He made a lot of people smile every day.

We wanted you to know a portion of the profits of this book will be donated in Bear's memory to local animal shelters, parks, conservation organizations, and other individuals and nonprofit organizations in need of assistance.

– Douglas & Sherri Brown

PS: We have since adopted two more rescue dogs: first Scout, and the following year, Ginger. They were both mixed golden retrievers who needed a home.

Want to help animals and the world? Here are a dozen easy suggestions you and your family can implement today:

- *Adopt and rescue a pet from a local shelter.*
- *Support local and no-kill animal shelters.*
- *Plant a tree to honor someone you love.*
- *Be a developer — put up some birdhouses.*
- *Buy live, potted Christmas trees and replant them.*
- *Make sure you spend time with your animals each day.*
- *Save natural resources by recycling and buying recycled products.*
- *Drink tap water, or filter your own water at home.*
- *Whenever possible, limit your use of or do not use pesticides.*
- *If you eat seafood, make sustainable choices.*
- *Support your local farmers market.*
- *Get outside. Visit a park, volunteer, walk your dog, or ride your bike.*

Five years ago, Atlantic Publishing signed the Green Press Initiative. These guidelines promote environmentally friendly practices, such as using recycled stock and vegetable-based inks, avoiding waste, choosing energy-efficient resources, and promoting a no-pulping policy. We now use 100-percent recycled stock on all our books. The results: in one year, switching to post-consumer recycled stock saved 24 mature trees, 5,000 gallons of water, the equivalent of the total energy used for one home in a year, and the equivalent of the greenhouse gases from one car driven for a year.

DEDICATION

This book is dedicated to Karen,
the real gardener in the family.

TABLE OF CONTENTS

INTRODUCTION

*W*hen one thinks about a garden and the activity of gardening, it is quite natural to think of digging into the dirt, pulling weeds, fertilizing, and composting. This book, *How to Grow Fruits, Vegetables & Houseplants Without Soil: The Secrets of Hydroponic Gardening Revealed*, will offer an alternative to the traditional notion that one requires a good plot of land with rich soil in a sunny location to be a successful gardener with a bountiful garden.

Hydroponic gardening is a dirt-free, low-cost, space saving, low in pesticides, and environmentally friendly way of growing plants without any soil. Once you understand the fundamentals of hydroponic gardening, you too will be able to reap the benefits of this easy-to-do horticultural alternative.

Hydroponic gardening does not require you be a professional horticulturalist. The purpose of this book is to help you to learn how to grow soil-free in your own home. This book will help you understand the fundamentals of soil-free growing. It will take you from understanding exactly what defines hydroponic gardening, to learning about the life-cycle of a plant, and what it takes to begin, nurture, and harvest plants of various types. You also will learn how to sustain your garden at the lowest cost possible by harvesting, not only the fruits of your labor, but also by gathering and saving seeds for new plants.

This book will serve as your is your step-by-step guide to learning how to set up your own hydroponic garden right in your backyard, greenhouse, or windowsill. You will learn about a wide variety of hydroponic gardening systems and how to deter-

mine which system may be right for you. You will learn about the range of equipment you might need for the system(s) you choose to employ. In some cases, you will be able to build your own equipment while in other cases, you will need to purchase equipment. This book will offer you resources no matter how you choose to proceed.

For those new to the practice of hydroponic gardening, this book will offer the simplest means possible to get started without designing, building, and/or purchasing equipment. The simple start practice will allow the beginner to get his/her feet wet to see if hydroponics is right for them. Alternatively, the book will describe a variety of hydroponic gardening methods and systems that may be of interest to those with some basic experience. Hopefully, the view of alternative hydroponic methods will spur the experienced gardener to experiment with new and different systems they had not considered before.

This is one of the few books on the subject of hydroponic gardening written for individuals that are absolute beginners. It is meant to be a step-by-step guide to the practice of hydroponic gardening. As such, it is suggested that the reader, especially the beginning gardener, start at the beginning and work through the book in the systematic step-by-step manner. The book is designed to offer an overview of hydroponics, including a short history of the practice, and then delve into the specifics that the gardener needs to understand. Each chapter builds upon the previous chapter in terms of understanding the practice of hydroponic gardening. The reader that takes this guide in a step-by-step manner will benefit the most in the understanding of what hydroponic gardening is and how it works.

Also included in this book are case studies that will introduce you to individuals who will offer inspiration and advice regarding hydroponic gardening. These individuals are professional growers and home gardeners just like the readers that have adopted hydroponic gardening. The case studies will discuss best practices, offer tips, and encouragement to the reader.

The goal of this book is to give you everything you need to know to get started growing the healthiest of foods and flowers in your own home hydroponic garden.

If you have children, get them involved in hydroponics. Hydroponics is a great way to help kids to understand the life cycles of a wide variety of living things. Besides the health benefits gardening can offer everyone, it can be a wonderful learning opportunity. Working with children in a garden provides a great opportunity to experience the wonder of the cycle of life. It is also just great family fun that you can eat and appreciate!

AN OVERVIEW OF HYDROPONIC GARDENING

Simply stated, hydroponic gardening is a way of growing plants without soil. More directly, hydroponic gardening is a way of growing plants using water as the singular method of nutrient delivery. You will see, in most instances, hydroponics defined using the words "without soil," but the most important thing to know about hydroponics is that "with water" is more vital than "without soil." The word "hydroponic" literally means "water works." The word "hydroponics" is derived from two Greek words: "hydro," meaning water, and "ponics" meaning labor or work. Thus, we might suggest that the practice of hydroponics in one in which we let the water do the work.

When we think of traditional gardening methods, we always think that soil is the important factor. This, however, is not necessarily the case.

Jean Anthelme Brillat-Savarin was a French gastronome who lived in the late 18th and early 19th century. He is quoted as saying "Vegetables, which are the lowest in the scale of living things,

are fed by roots, which, implanted in the native soil, select by the action of a peculiar mechanism, different subjects, which serve to increase and to nourish them." He is also more famously remembered for saying: "Tell me what you eat, and I will tell you what you are." Gastronomy is mentioned here because it is the science of food and eating. Gastronomy relates to hydroponics because hydroponics concerns the method by which plants "eat" or take in nutrients. Plants take in nutrients through their roots. It is not the soil that feeds the plants, but the solution that shares the soil with the roots. That solution is the water.

Historical Hydroponics

It is hard to say who discovered that hydroponics was a viable way of growing plants or how the practice of hydroponic gardening came into being, but it is known that hydroponic gardening has been around for thousands of years.

One of the seven wonders of the ancient world, the Hanging Gardens of Babylon, is considered a hydroponic gardening system. King Nebuchadnezzar constructed the hanging gardens for his wife in the ancient city of Babylonia (about 50 miles south of Baghdad, Iraq) around 600 B.C.

The ancient Greeks historians, Strabo (63 B.C. - A.D. 24) and Philo (20 B.C. - 50 A.D.), have left us some wonderful descriptions of this magnificent garden: "The Garden is quadrangular, and each side is four plethra long. It consists of arched vaults, which are located on checkered cube-like foundations... The ascent of the uppermost terrace-roofs is made by a stairway...

"The Hanging Garden has plants cultivated above ground level, and the roots of the trees are embedded in an upper terrace rather than in the earth. The whole mass is supported on stone columns... Streams of water emerging from elevated sources flow down sloping channels... These waters irrigate the whole garden saturating the roots of plants and keeping the whole area moist. Hence the grass is permanently green and the leaves of trees grow firmly attached to supple branches... For the root system is kept saturated and sucks up the all-pervading supply of water, wandering in interlaced channels beneath the ground, and securely maintaining the well-established and excellent quality of trees. This is a work of art of royal luxury, and its most striking feature is that the labor of cultivation is suspended above the heads of the spectators."

It is believed that a mechanism called an Archimedes screw was employed to carry about 8,000 gallons of water a day from the Euphrates River ground level up to the top of the garden more than 300 feet high.

Another example of early hydroponic gardening can be found on the highland plateau of central Mexico. The highland plateau is where metropolitan Mexico City is situated. It was here that the Aztecs practiced hydroponic gardening using a system known as "chinampas." Chinampas were floating gardens that some historians believe were begun as early as 1400 B.C., though there is no firm proof of them before about 1100 A.D. The word "chinampas" is derived from and very descriptive of the way in which the gardens were constructed. "Chinampas" is combined chinamitl (reed basket) and pan (upon). The gardens were constructed by draining an area of a lake. After the area was drained, reeds were woven over the area and the area was enclosed. The reed basket that was constructed above the lake bed was then filled with sediment from the lake bottom before the area was flooded again. In this case, the sediment was not used like soil, but more as an anchor for the bed. Crops such as maize, potatoes, amaranth, and chia were grown in these "floating gardens" that were constructed to help feed the hundreds of thousands of people that lived in the central Mexican plain.

The practice of growing plants in the manner of the Hanging Gardens of Babylon and the chinampas of the Mexican plains are just two early examples of hydroponic gardening. Aristotle, Marco Polo, and many others also have chronicled a wide variety of hydroponic gardening techniques from all over the world from

China, to Egypt, to South America, but it was not until the 1600s that the science of plant nutrition was examined and chronicled.

Belgian scientist, Jan van Helmont, was among the earliest researchers to record,

through scientific method, that plants obtain substances such as nutrients from water. Van Helmont planted a five-pound willow shoot in a vessel that contained 200 pounds of dried soil. The vessel was then covered to keep out any possible contaminants. Van Helmont regularly watered the contents of the vessel with rainwater for five years. After this period, he noted that the willow shoot had increased in weight by 160 pounds. Van Helmont also noted that the soil lost less than two ounces. The conclusion that Jan van Helmont drew from this observation was that plants grown in dirt receive their nutrients, not from the dirt, but from the water. It was subsequently realized, at a later date, that plants also benefit from the oxygen and carbon dioxide in the air around them.

In 1699 British scientist, John Woodward, determined that pure water was not as good for soilless plants when compared to water that once had soil soaked in it, which led to the important understanding of how water holds minerals once it has been in contact with soil. It was this research that led to the first man-made nutrient solution for hydroponic gardening.

The idea of trying to grow plants without soil really started to take hold in the early 1900s when several researchers at the University of California, Berkeley continued to work in this field and coin the term "hydroponics." In the late 1920s and early 1930s, Dr. William F. Gericke of the University of California broadened and expanded his indoor laboratory experimentation to include work on plant nutrition in a more practical nature by growing crops outside. Gericke called what he was working on "hydroponics." This was the first time the word was used to describe plants grown in a water system. Gericke's work is now thought to be the foundation for all methods of hydroponic gardening, even though it had been practiced for thousands of years before he came along.

The timeliness of Gericke's work also coincided with the rise in the use of greenhouses and in the use of refrigeration as a means of storing and transporting food grown in one part of the country and shipped to another. One of the primary locations for this explosion in agriculture meant to feed a growing country was the California valley near the University of California at Berkley. The use of greenhouses, hydroponics, and refrigeration gained in popularity to bring out-of-season produce to consumers for additional profit.

But the various experiments that went on at that time were of limited success due to the materials they had to work with (gravel, wood, concrete, glass). When plastic became a commonly available building material, interest picked back up, and new hydroponics system concepts were experimented with.

One of the first truly successful uses for hydroponics in growing food was in 1938 when Pan-Am Airways created a commercial operation on tiny Wake Island so that they could use the island as a restocking point for flights. Similar principles were applied on otherwise barren Pacific islands during World War II to produce food for the troops.

In more recent times, NASA has been doing more intensive experiments with hydroponics as a clean and efficient way to raise food plants in space. Not only can growing plants produce food, they also will clean the air and produce oxygen. All of these factors make this a valuable program for NASA and hopefully with more research, we can expect to see new breakthroughs in hydroponics in the near future. According to the NASA.gov website, they are learning more about how varying combinations of light, nutrients, and carbon dioxide impact plant growth. They also are looking at improving yields by combining certain plants instead of only growing one crop at a time.

The Basic "How" and "Why" of Hydroponic Gardening

All hydroponics systems have a different way of functioning, but they all have a few concepts in common with each other. The very basic premise is that plants are grown with their roots exposed and suspended in some way (usually in an inorganic growing medium, such as vermiculite or clay pellets). The exposed roots are fed a water-based nutrient solution in order to feed and nourish the plants. The specific method for keeping the roots soaked in nutrients is how each system will vary from another.

Some systems will keep your plants continually immersed in a nutrient solution, and others run on timers to flood your roots at certain points of the day. Another option is to supply them constantly with only a thin stream of flowing liquid at the root tips. Still others will use a misting system for continual delivery of nutrients to the roots through the air. More on these different approaches can be found in

Chapter 2. They all have their positives and negatives, usually involving their cost and complexity.

A plant's roots are designed to take in water and water-soluble minerals. It is that nutrition that they need, not the soil itself. They will easily take in the solution that you provide without having to alter how a plant naturally functions.

Because some systems are maintained indoors, they also include lighting. Large banks of fluorescent lights are used to mimic the proper wavelength of sunlight. Though this is distinctly separate from the water systems, it is a vital part of the overall hydroponics setup.

Some hydroponic systems can be designed for outdoor use. These systems make it more difficult to control the environmental factors of light, humidity, and airflow.

Pros and cons

You should consider the pros and cons of each system carefully before making any decisions about how to proceed. These pros and cons will vary from person to person and situation to situation. What works for one individual will not work for another. Several common threads on the pro side apply to any type of hydroponic system:

Control

Hydroponic gardening allows the gardener to be in greater control over his or her garden than what conventional outdoor soil based gardening will allow. With hydroponics, you will be able to provide mineral nutrients in the precise combination and mixture that you feel will best suit your plants. Also, if you have an indoor system, you can modify and adjust the lighting to various points on the spectrum to further fine-tune your gardening. If you like to tweak even the tiniest variable to try and improve your production, then you really should try hydroponics.

Cleanliness

Without soil, you will find that hydroponics is somewhat less messy than soil gardening. This may not be as important as other issues unless you are trying to garden indoors in a small space. Being able to avoid the dirt can be a significant positive if you are trying to grow plants in the corner of the living room or even in a closet. Your indoor system also will lower the risk of your plants being eaten by pests. There will be fewer insects with a hydroponics system, though this particular problem is not eliminated completely.

Increased productivity

Your indoor hydroponic garden, fed by a well-balanced mix of nutrients under optimum lighting, will not be subject to the whims of nature. Thus, you can expect to get high productivity out of your plants. Your growth results per square foot will be greater than outdoor soil-based gardening, and there will be fewer losses due to pests.

Growing out of season

Technically, off-season growing also would apply to any soil gardening that is done in a greenhouse, but it remains a decent positive side to hydroponics compared to outdoor soil-based gardens. With an indoor garden that is under your control for light and temperature, you can have crops from any plants regardless of whether they normally would grow in your region. Fresh fruit and vegetables can be harvested in the middle of winter. You no longer have to time all of your gardening by the seasons or calendar. After each harvest, you immediately can start a new batch of seedlings for the next crop.

Efficient water usage

While it may seem like a lot of water is used when growing plants hydroponically, it actually uses less water than conventional soil gardening because of the lack of waste and the ability to recycle the water (adding more nutrients when necessary). Outdoors, in a soil-based garden, much of the water that goes into the soil eventually soaks in beyond the reach of your plants roots or is otherwise drained away and unused. This one fact alone is motivating further research and development into hydroponics in dry climates or areas hit by drought. Being able to grow crops with less water is a huge positive in any scenario, as long as your hydroponics arrangement recycles as much as possible.

But even with these substantial positives, there are still a few negatives to running a hydroponic garden. You should be just as equally aware of these.

Cost

Yes, you easily can spend several hundred dollars putting a system together, but you do not necessarily have to. Many parts of a hydroponics system can be put together yourself with very inexpensive supplies from your neighborhood hardware store. Many of the system descriptions in Chapter 4 will include ways to cut costs by doing some of the building yourself. You could put together a small one-plant system to experiment with for under $20 if you stick to the simple designs and buy your parts at the hardware or pet store.

You should remember that all of the equipment costs are up front and mostly a one-time investment. Nutrient solutions will have to be purchased regularly though.

Another part of indoor hydroponic gardening systems that may add to their cost is the expense of the electrical power necessary to operate lights and fans. Having large lights on through the day, as well as electrical timers, pumps, fans, and more can be a sizable burden on your electric bill. Many people feel this is off-set by the increased productivity, particularly if you are growing your own food.

Time and effort

Most parts of a hydroponic system will be automatic. With a few good timers, you can run your pumps without actually having to be around to do the chores yourself. This does reduce your work-load but you still can expect to have to watch your plants closely on a very regular basis. Nutrient solutions have to be monitored and remixed/refilled; plants need to be watched for any prob-lems or deficiencies; and many other factors need to be moni-tored as well. You have to keep track of CO_2 levels, temperatures, lighting, and more. This is the negative side of the control coin. Thankfully, you can decide for yourself how "hands on" you want to be with daily chores and choose a system or technique that will minimize your effort.

All things considered, you will be able to make your hydroponic gardening systems as simple or as complex as you are capable of supporting. A system can be as simple as a jar of water or as complex as a greenhouse filled with artificial lighting systems, timed misting devices, pumps, and humidifiers. You can purchase a ready-made hydroponic gardening system, or you can design and build your own system.

Good advice for those brand new to hydroponic gardening is to start small, learn the ropes, and build a little at a time. Let your desire to expand and learn more be fuelled by your successes, failures, and inspirations.

Range of Hydroponic Gardening Systems

As mentioned earlier, hydroponic gardening systems can be as simple as a jar of water. Hydroponic gardening systems also can be highly complex. Truly, how you plan to begin and grow your hydroponic gardening system is only limited by your creativity, desire, and means. To some extent, the system you eventually end up with will be dictated by what you would like to grow. Some systems are better suited for growing particular types of plants than others. You might employ a different hydroponic gardening system to grow carrots than you would to grow tomatoes. The following review of basic hydroponic gardening systems will include some suggestions for the kinds of plants that might be better suited for the particular types of systems. Later chapters will go into more detail about the specifics of the systems, their designs, operations, and the kinds of plants that are suitable.

The simple jar

Perhaps, the best place to start your adventure in hydroponic gardening is simply to grow some sprouts. Sprouts, grown in a jar of water, are the most basic form of plants grown hydroponically. You do not need to build any systems, invest in any equipment, or spend a whole lot of time to grow seeds that will provide you with a basic education and a great deal of nutrition.

You can grow a whole host of seeds to sprouts in a simple jar of water, from beans, to grains, and vegetables. Sprouted seeds, beans, and nuts can be eaten raw or used to cook with in an infinite number of ways.

All you need to get started growing your own sprouts is a jar, seeds, and water. You can happily and easily grow large amounts of sprouts for many years with only those three items. The jar you choose is not a specially designed jar for sprouting; any glass jar will do. The best jars are quart-sized, wide-mouth canning jars. You can use any wide-mouth glass jar. The size of the jar will determine the amount of seeds that you will be able to sprout. Keep in mind the larger the jar, the greater your sprouting capabilities.

Sprouting seeds in a jar is simply a matter of soaking the seeds and making sure that you change the water regularly. Start your sprouts in a dark place, and as they begin to form, move the jar into indirect sunlight to allow them to green a little. It is that easy.

Six Rules and Steps of Jar Sprouting

1. Rinse frequently.	4. Sprouts need plenty of breathing room.
2. Keep sprouts moist (not wet).	5. Don't over fill the sprout container.
3. Keep sprouts at room temperature.	6. Keep sprouts covered and in the dark.
Step One: Soaking Use 1½ tablespoons of seeds in a quart-sized jar. Screw on the fine mesh lid and partially fill the jar with warm water. Swirl to clean the seeds then pour out. Refill with warm water to cover at 3 times their depth and soak overnight, away from light.	**Step two: Draining and Starting** Pour off the water. Place drained jar in a dark place, propped at an angle to allow any extra water to drain out. Turn the jar to spread out the seeds. Cover the jar with a towel and leave for 3 to 4 hours.
Step Three: Rinsing Rinse sprouts with cool, fresh water 2 or 3 times daily until they are ready to eat. When they begin to throw off the seed hulls, let the jar overflow with water and the hulls will float out the top through the screen. Turn the jar to spread out the seeds with each rinse.	**Step Four: Harvesting** Pour the sprouts into clean water in a pan or sink. Remaining hulls will float to the surface. Skim off. Remove the sprouts, gently shake off excess moisture and drain in a colander.

Six Rules and Steps of Jar Sprouting	
Step Five: Greening After cleaning the jar and lid, return sprouts for greening back to the jar. Place in indirect sunlight, such as near a window. After the sprouts have greened (about a day) rinse, drain, and eat or refrigerate.	Step Six: Refrigeration Sprouts will stay fresh in the refrigerator for a week if they are rinsed daily. To keep at their nutritional peak, give green sprouts an extra hour of sunlight after rinsing. Sprouts are frost sensitive, so keep them away from freezer compartment.

You will learn about several hydroponic gardening systems in Chapter 4 that are only slightly more complex than this simple sprouting garden. Systems such as the bubbler system and the bucket system are, fundamentally, based on the same notion as the sprout jar. The differences in the systems are predicated on the changing needs of the plant as it grows from seed, to sprout, shoot, and fully mature plant.

You can consider several basic hydroponic gardening systems beyond the simple sprout in a jar system. Following are the working theories of each system. Chapter 4 covers the specifics of each system.

There are, essentially, two basic types of hydroponic gardening systems: static systems and dynamic systems. There are a number of varieties of each of these two types of systems. The difference between the two types of systems is somewhat described in their names. Static systems do not allow for the circulation of water. Dynamic systems allow water to circulate. The sprouting jar described earlier is a static hydroponic growing system.

Static Hydroponic Growing Systems

Static hydroponic systems are most easily started and are the primary choice of the beginning small-scale hydroponic gardener. When you choose to begin a static hydroponic gardening system, you will choose either an open system or a closed system. The difference between the two systems is that in an open hydroponic gardening system, the nutrient solution fed to the plants is not recovered. In a closed hydroponic gardening system, the nutrient solution is recovered and used as long as the nutrient solution is viable and beneficial to the plants.

Because of the simple nature of the static solution system, you can create them in several ways. The main two forms of this nature are the raft system and the bucket system. Raft systems have plants floating on the surface of the aerated water solution, and bucket systems have the plants held in place. Bucket systems tend to be smaller and are used for individual plants or small groupings. The water does not flow, which makes this a simpler system to use and set up because it needs less equipment.

The primary types of static hydroponic gardening systems are:

- Raft system
- Bucket system
- Top-drip system
- Wick system
- Ebb-and-flow system (note: the ebb-and-flow system can be either a static or dynamic system, depending on how you treat the nutrient solution after it flows away from the plants. If the solution is not recirculated through the system, the system would be considered a static system. If the nutrient solution is recirculated through the system, the system is considered to be dynamic.)

Raft systems

This is most commonly used with lettuce, herbs, and other small leafy plants. The main reason for this is that the plants have to float on the surface of the solution, and larger plants make this

impractical. The main pieces of equipment are floating components to hold your plants on the surface of the solution and a
large container to use as a reservoir. You also need an aerator
because the water is not moving.

You get a little more flexibility with your plants because they are
not fastened in place like they are in most other systems. You
easily can add another plant or two with additional floatation
pieces. Some systems have one single floating piece with holes
for the individual plants and some have each plant floating inde-
pendently. To keep your plants floating, mesh pots can be placed
in pieces of Styrofoam®.

A large plastic box or Rubbermaid® tote can be used for the reservoir, and any standard rigid Styrofoam from a home renovation
store will work as a flotation device.

Raft System Diagram

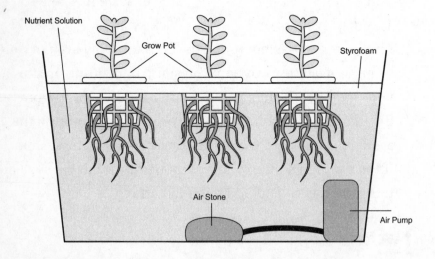

Bucket systems

This is sometimes called a deep water culture because it has a much deeper reservoir of water than some of the other types. Each bucket needs a support for the plant, which is usually a net basket for growing medium attached to the underside lid of the reservoir and a bubbler. A bucket system can be very basic, often using Rubbermaid totes as the main reservoir. This is good place to start if you plan on going the DIY route, much like the raft system.

The roots grow through the medium and mesh basket directly into the pool of liquid below in the reservoir. The solution is already aerated due to the bubbler, and the top portion of the roots is suspended above the liquid for additional breathing space.

Simple Bucket System Diagram

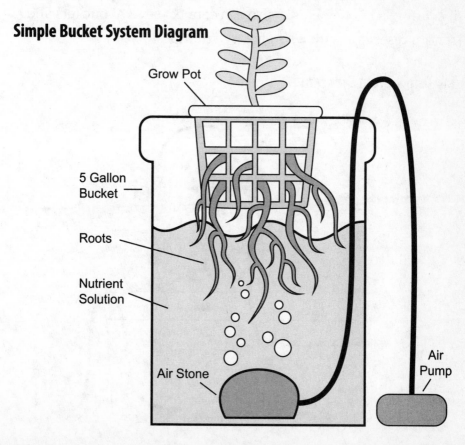

Grow Pot

5 Gallon Bucket

Roots

Nutrient Solution

Air Stone

Air Pump

Top drip

This is not strictly a static system, since the water is moving but it is closer to this style than any of the others. With a top drip, water is pumped from the bottom of the reservoir to above the plant support and growing medium. It then trickles down through the roots back to the reservoir. It is a continual loop. Bubblers are not needed because the constant motion of the water allows for natural aeration to take place and the water will not stagnate.

Aside from the top/bottom bucket arrangement, you also will need a pump with hosing to move the water from the bottom to the top. This is a very common type of hydroponic system, and it can be expanded to work with large trays of plants rather than just a single bucket. Hoses also can connect several buckets and a central reservoir with a single large pump.

Top Drip System Diagram

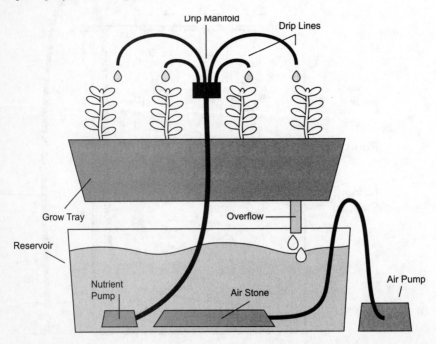

Wick systems

Wick systems are really the simplest type of hydroponics as they have no pumps or moving parts at all. Nutrient solution is drawn up from a small reservoir under your plants, into the main pot with the growing medium. Cloth strips or even short lengths of cotton rope are used as the wicks. Alternatively, the medium itself can be in contact with the water, and it will absorb naturally on its own. This approach will lead to wetter medium compared to the use of actual wicks.

This method is more like conventional "dirt gardening" because the plants roots usually are held completely within the mass of growing medium rather than exposed to the nutrient solution directly. The medium that you use for these types of arrangements must be absorbent (vermiculite, coco fiber, or moss) but also will need to have enough drainage throughout to allow for some air. The medium will stay constantly wet and can drown the roots otherwise.

The main benefit of using a wick system is the simplicity and the independence from a power source. Unlike the other options, this one will continue working just fine even if there is a prolonged power outage. Nutrient solution is not reclaimed or recycled through the system. You just have to refill the reservoir when the volume gets low.

A lack of air content for the roots makes this a less adequate choice for many plants though. Adding a bubbler to the reservoir can help, but once the water has soaked up through the wicks and the medium, most air content will be gone.

Wick System Diagram

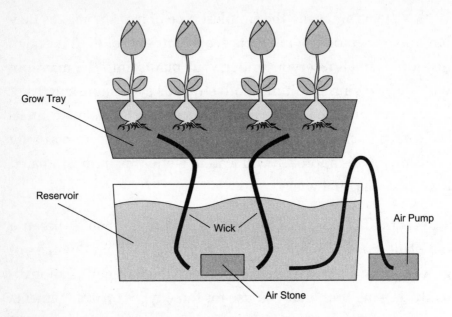

Dynamic Hydroponic Growing Systems

As mentioned earlier, dynamic hydroponic gardening systems are those systems that recirculate the liquid nutrient solution through the system as long as the system is viable.

Ebb and flow

This system creates a tidal effect, periodically flooding the root chambers with nutrient solution and then letting it drain back away. They also sometimes are called a flood-and-drain system. These are the most common systems for larger gardens once you have gone past the initial beginner stage. After the trays in which the plants are situated are flooded, the nutrient solution is allowed to drain. The drained nutrient solution in this dynamic system is collected and recirculated as long as the nutrient solution is viable.

Each of the systems mentioned above can be designed as open or closed systems, depending on how you choose to deal with nutrient solution. Chapter 4 will discuss, in greater detail, the specific designs of each of these static systems.

Nutrient film technique

This type of hydroponic arrangement is more commonly known as just NFT. The system is a little more advanced and not usually attempted by beginners until they have a little more knowledge about hydroponic equipment.

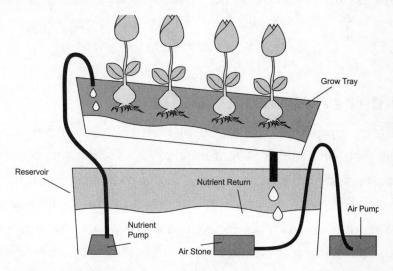

A thin film of water is pumped continually past the ends of the roots giving your plants a regular supply of nutrients while also leaving most of the root mass exposed to the air. This prevents drowning of the roots that can happen in too much water.

Aeroponics

An aeroponic approach is significantly different than the others because you are not working with liquid nutrient solutions in the same way. Your plants are suspended in their mesh pots but their roots hang loose in a large open chamber. Frequently through the day, solution is misted or sprayed into the chamber to nourish and moisten the roots.

Aeroponic systems are included here as a dynamic system because the more sophisticated aeroponic systems will recirculate the nutrient rich mist that feeds the plants with a system of pumps and fans.

Like the other systems noted above, you can choose not to recirculate the nutrient solution, but as aeroponics is somewhat more advanced than the simpler form of hydroponic gardening, it has been included here as a dynamic system.

Range of Hydroponic Media

Though your plants will get all of their nutrients from the solutions you provide, they still have to have some sort of physical support for their roots. There are many different options for this; some are organic, and some are man-made. In many cases, there are minimal difference between one type and the next even though many hydroponic gardeners may swear by one medium over another. You might have to do a little trial-and-error research to see what works best for you.

Before making a choice, you will need to know the basic features that a good growing medium should have. Fundamentally, all materials will be light and porous so that they can hold a mix of air and water within them and still allow for roots to grow freely between the particles. They also should be chemically inert so that they do not contribute to the nutrient mix that your solution is providing. That would defeat the main purpose of hydroponics.

A selection of materials is listed below, and there will be further discussion regarding this topic in Chapter 5, but there is no limit to what you can work with. If you have access to similar but unlisted materials, feel free to experiment. Also, there are many benefits to mixing two or more of these materials together to get the perfect conditions for your plants.

You will want to consider the absorbency of your medium and what kind of hydroponic gardening system you are going to employ. Some systems rely on the medium to *hold* water between pump runs, so you should keep that in mind. Common hydroponic gardening system growing media includes:

- Sand
- Expanded clay
- Perlite
- Rock wool
- Vermiculite
- Coconut fibre
- Oasis cubes

Hydroponic Nutrient solution

The water used in hydroponic gardening is, primarily, a nutrient delivery system. You will recall that earlier in this chapter in the section related to the history of hydroponic gardening, that British scientist, John Woodward, determined that pure water was not as good for soilless plants when compared to water that once had soil soaked in it, which led to the important understanding of how water holds minerals once it has been in contact with soil. It was this research that led to the first man-made nutrient solution for hydroponic gardening. Woodward's research in 1699 held true. Most water does not have adequate amounts of the specific nutrients necessary to support the life cycle of a plant, so you will be required to add nutrients to the water in your hydroponic gardening system. Chapter 6 will offer greater detail regarding plant nutrients. Specific formulas of nutrient solutions employed by hydroponic gardeners will be discussed in greater detail, and you will learn that different plants, like different people, may require and benefit from different nutrient solutions. The chapter also will include a section on fertilizers. Plants, like people, also may exhibit symptoms of nutritional deficiencies. As a hydroponic gardener, you will need to know how to spot these deficiencies and how to alter the plant's nutrition to deal with problems as they occur.

Taking the First Step

For the reader that is an absolute beginner to the practice of hydroponic gardening systems, it is advised that the best way to begin is to start small. Whether "small" means starting by growing a few sprouts in a jar or putting together a small inexpensive do-it-yourself system, a small step at the beginning will help the reader understand the overall process; what it entails; the amount of time; the space requirements; and many other issues that may arise in beginning a new venture.

The following chapters of this book are meant to take the reader, step-by-step, through the process of understanding and beginning a home hydroponic gardening system. The book will start at the very beginning of the process by discussing horticulture in general and move to the specifics of hydroponic systems, the equipment needed to construct them, and the knowledge and materials needed to sustain them.

GARDENING

I used to visit and revisit it a dozen times a day, and stand in deep contemplation over my vegetable progeny with a love that nobody could share or conceive of who had never taken part in the process of creation. It was one of the most bewitching sights in the world to observe a hill of beans thrusting aside the soil, or a rose of early peas just peeping forth sufficiently to trace a line of delicate green.

~ **Nathaniel Hawthorne**, *Mosses from an Old Manse*

If you are a gardener, or know a gardener, you understand the passion of Nathaniel Hawthorne's statement. Gardeners have a passion for life and things that grow. Gardeners appreciate the life of their gardens no matter whether they are grown to be viewed, smelled, or eaten. Gardens provide the soul of the gardener solace unlike that found anywhere else.

"Gardening is cheaper than therapy, and you get tomatoes."

~**Author Unknown**

Gardening, like many other pursuits, has its own special mindset and its own special language. Each gardener develops a garden that might well define the personality and particular character of the individual that creates it. Some would argue that once the garden has been created, the garden then shapes the gardener as the plants, fruit,

vegetable, or flower, molds the actions of the gardener to their own (the plant's own) needs. Whether the gardener has created a soil-based garden, a hydroponic garden, or and aeroponic garden, once the life-cycle has begun, the gardener, the plants, and the surrounding environment all seem to become dependent on each other to support their varied needs.

Horticulture

Horticulture is defined as the science and art of growing and using fruits, vegetables, flowers, ornamental plants, and grasses to improve our environment and to diversify our diets. The science and art of horticulture includes an understanding of the sciences of biology, chemistry, and ecology. Horticulturists need to have an understanding of air and water, as well an understanding of the complete environmental surroundings that include, not only air and water, but also all other life in the given environment.

The term "horticulture," as defined above, also includes the word "art." This implies that the horticulturist is not only concerned with knowledge, as classically defined through the term "science," but also is concerned with creation via human expression and the communication of such expression by the individual or community. Horticulture differs from botany in that botany, strictly speaking, is the scientific study of plant life.

Gardeners, whether they are professional horticulturists or home gardeners, learn, usually from experiencing their particular environment, all factors that play into the life of their garden. Through experience, home gardeners become home-grown horticulturists. Gardening becomes an expression of the life of the gardener and their immediate environment.

The Seed

"To see things in the seed, that is genius."

— **Lao Tzu**, *Chinese philosopher*

Whether the seed is a seed of thought or a mustard seed, a seed is a beginning, as well as an ending. A seed is part of an ongoing life cycle: the seed grows into the plant that produces the seed and on and on. What power that little seed must hold. We all know the proverb, "From little acorns, mighty oaks do grow." This sentiment is just as true of sunflower seeds, wheat berries, and lentils, all of which hold the power of transformation.

The first step each of these seeds, grains, legumes, and nuts take in this life cycle of transformation is to become a sprout. To **sprout** is to begin to grow from a seed, grain, legume, or nut. As this book proceeds, those will be our categories of designation.

The sprout is the first stage of life beyond the seed. Seeds are dormant packets of energy; that is, they are asleep. Seeds can remain  dormant for very long periods. In fact, scientists are still trying to answer the question of just how long seeds can remain dormant. Scientists have sprouted seeds that they know for a fact are 140 years old. UCLA research biologist Jane Shen-Miller has a living seed from a dry lake bed in China that has been dated using carbon testing as being more than 1,200 years old. A **living seed** is a seed that, while still dormant, is capable of sprouting.

All this points to a life force within a seed that is powerful and resilient. A sprout occurs the moment that dormant life force has been awakened. Sprouts of seeds, grains, legumes, and nuts require the life-giving power of water for this awakening. Hungarian biochemist Albert Szent-György, who won the 1937 Nobel Prize for Medicine, is quoted as saying: "Water is life's matter and matrix, mother, and medium. There is no life without water." That is as true for humans as it is for seeds, grains, legume, and nuts.

To sprout a seed, you need to just add water. To test this, do a little experiment. Take one seed, any kind of seed will do, and drop it in a glass of water. Place the glass in a dark place, and after a few days (depending on the kind of seed you choose), a sprout will appear. Some seeds, grains, legumes, or nuts transform overnight. Red lentils will show sprouts in as little as 12 hours.

How a seed transforms into a sprout is a very complex tale that begins before the seed itself is produced. As the seed is a part of a cycle of life, saying that the seed comes before the plant is akin to saying that the egg came before the chicken. The seed was born by a plant that put all of its life's energies into making seeds. Making seeds ensures the plant will continue to thrive from generation to generation. In making the seed, the plant stored all the vitamins, minerals, proteins, fats, and carbohydrates necessary to give birth to another of its species. The plant packs the seed and casts it off to wait for just the right time and environment suitable for germination. To **germinate** is to sprout, and to sprout is to begin the life cycle anew.

As a gardener, your task is to provide the environment suitable for germination and life. By providing that seed with "life's matter and matrix," that is, water and air at a proper temperature, you allow that seed to begin to transform that stored energy into a growing life force.

Transforming from Seed to Sprout

How to set the life cycle in motion for seeds, grains, legumes, and nuts varies from seed to seed. Seeds, grains, legumes, and nuts all vary in their means of germination, depending on how the plant developed over its long history as a living organism. Some seeds have thin outer coats and will germinate very quickly with a little water and a relatively warm temperature. However, some seeds that require a longer germination time were developed to be ingested by animals, carried away from the plant that produced it, and dispersed far away after a long winter. Some seeds have developed a deep dormancy that protects the seed from sprouting in the late fall or winter, which would certainly not be beneficial to its continued survival. Some nuts, such as almonds, have very thin seed coats and require a very short germination time (one to two days). The other end of the spectrum is the coconut, with a very thick coat, that takes about four months to sprout.

As the seed is sprouted, some very significant chemical changes begin to take place. The seed, with the help of water and air, begins to produce enzymes that are vital in converting the stored and concentrated nutrients into everything the seed will need to carry on the life cycle. **Enzymes** are proteins produced in living cells that speed up or increase the rate of a chemical reaction such as the metabolic processes of an organism. Enzymes can increase the speed of a chemical reaction by up to a million times more than normal. By introducing that little seed to water, you have set a miraculous force into motion.

The enzymes cause many changes as a seed sprouts: The stored carbohydrates are being transformed into simple sugars; complex proteins are being turned into amino acids; fatty acids, vitamins, and minerals are all increasing at incredible rates; and the sprout takes minerals and other elements from the water and binds them to amino acids. All of these very complex activities are done to continue the plant's life cycle.

Before you learn how to grow the little powerhouses that transform from seeds, to sprouts, to shoots, and then into maturing plants that produce more seeds, it is important that you know what exactly is going on inside that seed that makes it sprout. To understand the anatomy of the seed is to understand its genius.

Anatomy of a Seed

The true blessing of the seed is the miracle of what the seed holds. It was stated previously that plants live to create those seeds, grains, legumes, and nuts that will ensure their survival as a species. While it is true that not all plants produce seeds to reproduce, this section will examine plants that produce seeds; how those seeds are produced; how the seeds are dispersed; and how the seeds germinate to begin the life cycle anew.

In examining the entirety of the plant kingdom that produces seeds, you can separate those plants into two categories: plants that produce flowers and those that do not produce flowers. There is a category of plant that does not produce flowers or seeds (ferns, for example), and these plants reproduce via spores. A wide variety of plants produce flowers, including apple trees, cacti, and pumpkins. Seed-bearing plants that do not produce flowers include coniferous trees like spruce trees and pine trees.

Pollination

Both flowering and non-flowering seed-producing plants follow a similar growth process, and both kinds of plants have male and female  parts. Plants produce pollen (the male part) and a way to collect the pollen, such as a flower or, in the case of coniferous trees, cones (the female part). The wind, insects, or animals transfer pollen from plant to plant to fertilize the female part of the plant. After fertilization, seeds are produced.

Coniferous trees rely solely on the wind for pollination. The pollen is very light and light breezes can easily transport it. The cones of trees are sticky and easily catch the pollen that blows in the wind.

Flowering plants may be pollinated by pollen in the wind, but they also rely on bees, other insects, and animals as well. As bees gather nectar from flowers, they also gather pollen on their bodies, and this pollen travels with them from plant to plant. Pollen fertilizes the plant, and after the plant is fertilized, it creates seeds. Fertilized flowering plants create seeds in fruit and coniferous plants create the seed in their cones. The fruit and the cone are used to protect the seed. In that seed is all the genetic information and plant energy required to make a new plant. When the seed matures to the point that it has collected all the information and energy that is required to grow a new plant, the mother plant casts the seed off to do its job of sprouting, growing, and keeping the cycle of life moving forward.

Because most plants are stationary and cannot travel from place to place, they count on animals and the wind to scatter their seeds. Sometimes the seed falls close to the mother plant, but sometimes a bird may eat the fruit containing the seed and fly a great distance to drop the seed many miles away. Or sometimes the seed is harvested for you to use in your kitchen and sprouting jar.

Seeds for sprouting come from flowering plants and coniferous plants. Some seeds sprout better than others, and all seeds are not germinated in the same way, but all seeds are of a similar design, and each viable seed has the ability to grow on to become a new plant, given the right conditions.

Germination

The best kind of seed to examine as you explore how a seed germinates is a bean. Beans are large compared to other seeds, and it is relatively easy to open them and see what is going on inside. Also, beans have relatively thin coats, making them easy to open.

To see how a bean germinates, fold and roll a thick paper towel so it conforms to the inside of a clear glass. Put some sand in the middle of the paper towel in the glass to hold the paper towel in its cylindrical shape as you will be wetting the towel. Place a bean (kidney or lima beans work well for this experiment) between the paper towel and the glass, so you can see the bean. Moisten the paper towel with water. Place the glass in a dark cabinet, and observe it over several days. You will see the bean sprout develop a root and begin to develop leaves.

To make this experiment a little more illustrative as to what is happening in that bean, take a second bean, and slice it open to look inside. See what it looks like inside before it germinates. To make it easier to open, soak the bean overnight, which will cause it to soften and swell a little. Make a cut around the outer edge of the bean, avoiding the blemish where the bean was connected by the seed stalk to the inside of the pod. If you are using a larger bean like a lima bean, you should be able to identify this blemish. After you make the cut, you easily can remove the seed coat, which is called the testa. As you remove the testa, you will see a young root (called a radicle) that fits into the area alongside that small blemish you did not cut. This is where the seed was attached to the pod. You might liken this to an umbilical cord because this is how the seed received nutrients from the mother plant.

You will find that you can split the inside of the bean into two halves, which are called the **cotyledons**. The cotyledons are the seed leaves and contain the stored energy the seed will need to grow into a plant. In other words, the cotyledon is the plant's food. Between the cotyledons is the tiny plant that will develop into a new bean plant. This is the tiny plant that you will see emerge from the bean in your glass experiment. This tiny plant is made up of a root and a **plumule** (shoot) that has small leaves.

After the mother plant has cast off the seed, its germination depends on the temperature and moisture of the environment in which it eventually lands. Warmer temperatures are generally more conducive to germination and seed growth. The germination process consists of the seed taking on water, which triggers the production of enzymes that convert the stored and concentrated nutrients into all the things the seed will need to carry on the life cycle. *This process was described earlier in this chapter.*

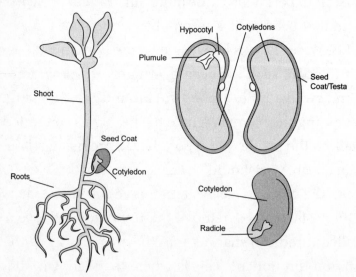

Sprouts versus Shoots

As the seed feeds itself and that feeding increases, a root pushes through the testa. The root is the part of the plant that, if set in soil, travels down into the earth to anchor the plant and collect nutrients from the soil. This is a sprout. The water causes new growth to occur in the seed, which forms the sprout.

The part of the seed that will travel upward to collect nutrients from the sun and the air is the plumule. The plumule, if allowed to develop, will become a **shoot**. Thus, the new growth that will become the root is the sprout, and the aerial part of the plant that will become a leaf is the shoot.

A seed that is not set in soil will still send roots out to anchor as well as gather nutrients. Many types of hydroponic systems require the growers to provide various growing media that are used to help anchor the plants as well as to retain nutrient solution. These media will be discussed at greater detail in Chapter 6.

Plant Strategies

After the seed has sprouted and grown into a shoot, the plant will assume a strategy its particular variety has developed over time to grow into a mature plant and bear seeds that will ensure the continuation of its specific species. There are more than 300,000 species of plants in the world, each having developed its own strategy for survival based on the environment in which it developed. Many of the plants in that number have been domesticated, but the argument has been made that domestication is part of the plant's strategy for survival.

Author Michael Pollan, in his book *The Botany of Desire*, makes the case that plants such as corn, apple trees, potatoes, and hemp have done as much to "domesticate" humans as humans have done to domesticate them. Pollan argues that humans act as "bumble bees" to aid in the pollination of these plants and have aided in their desire to survive as a species.

As a gardener, whether you choose to plant your seeds in soil or you engage in hydroponic gardening, part of your job is to understand the strategy that the seeds you have planted have developed to survive over the millennia. If you are successful at understanding these varied strategies, you are sure to have a bountiful garden.

Chapter 3

HYDRO

*a*s defined in Chapter 1, the word "hydroponics" is derived from two Greek words: "hydro", meaning water; "ponics" meaning labor or work. In other words: We let the water do the work. Water is, perhaps, the most important component of any hydroponic gardening system. Also know that most plants are about 75 percent water. You, as a hydroponic gardener, should examine a number of factors when you decide whether to use your home tap water for gardening purposes, and if you choose to do so, what you might do to make it better for your plants. You should know how hard or soft your water is, and you should have a feel for the general chemical composition of your water.

A good place to start to get a feel for the quality of your water is to do a pH test. According to the Environmental Protection Agency, "The pH scale measures how acidic or basic a substance is. It ranges from 0 to 14. A pH of 7 is neutral. A pH less than 7 is acidic, and a pH greater than 7 is basic. Each whole pH value below 7 is ten times more acidic than the next higher value. For example, a pH of 4 is ten times more acidic than a pH of 5 and 100 times (ten times ten) more acidic than a pH of 6. The same holds true for pH values above 7, each of which is ten times more alkaline — another way to say basic — than the next lower whole value. For example, a pH of 10 is ten times more alkaline than a pH of 9.

"Pure water is neutral, with a pH of 7.0. When chemicals are mixed with water, the mixture can become either acidic or basic. Vinegar and lemon juice are acidic substances, while laundry detergents and ammonia are basic." You can purchase pH test kits at most large hardware stores.

You also might want to know how hard your water is. Hard water is measured by the amount of mineral salts that exist in it. You can get a report on the hardness of your home's water from your municipal water service. You can get kits at your local hardware store that will test your water. You will see on the table below numbers that correspond to the water's alkalinity and hardness.

Needless to say, you probably want to start with water that is as close to neutral as possible. If you are really curious to find out about the state of the water you are using from your tap, you can probably go to your city's municipal website and search for a water quality report issued by your local water system. The following information was included in an annual water report submitted by the City of Lincoln, Nebraska. The report also offers the note at the end that "Lincoln's water is moderately hard."

Water Quality Parameters

pH (in pH units) 7.71

Total Alkalinity (CaCO) 3160 ppm

Total Hardness (CaCO) 3200 ppm

(12 grains per gallon)

Total Dissolved Solids 336 ppm

Calcium 54.4 ppm

Chloride 20.5 ppm

Iron <0.05 ppm
Manganese 1.04 ppb
Sodium 30.6 ppm
Sulfate 77 ppm
(12/10/09)

Lincoln's water is moderately hard. Alkalinity, pH and hardness are important if considering a water softener.

Of the items listed in the water report above, six will have the greatest impact on gardening: carbonate (noted on the above table as Total Alkalinity), chloride, sodium, calcium, sulfate, and magnesium.

Again, remember that various plants have developed a variety of strategies for their growth and survival. In the same way, they have developed a variety of "tastes" and "preferences" for different chemical compositions that aid in their nutrition. A good example is the blueberry bush that requires a highly acidic environment to grow and produce fruit. The fruit of the blueberry, at the same time, contains a skin that is also highly acidic.

On a water report, you will often see these items listed in parts per million (ppm), which is equivalent to 1 milligram per liter (mg/L). To convert the ppm listed on your local water report to mg/L, you can go to **www.unitconversion.org/concentration-solution/part-per-million-ppm-conversion.html**. This website, UnitConversion.org, provides many online conversion tools and resources.

Local tap water can be diluted with purified or distilled water to adjust your target water profile. Also, you can use additives to increase the level of key minerals. Additives of choice are baking soda ($NaHCO_3$), table salt ($NaCl$), gypsum ($CaSO_4$), calcium chloride ($CaCl$), epsom salts ($MgSO_4$), and chalk ($CaCO_3$).

Adjusting the hardness and pH of your water for the purpose of hydroponic gardening is a complicated matter, but it is good to know the state of your water. For beginning gardeners, if you have water that falls way outside the range of neutral in pH, hardness, and/or taste, you might consider gardening with neutral purified or spring water. The cost of five gallons of water is not prohibitive, and you will be much more assured and happier with the results you will achieve rather than the ones you will achieve with unsatisfactory water. Of course, if you have a large-scale growing operation, this cost may be prohibitive.

When you think about altering the chemical composition of your local water supply, you also will need to keep in mind the nutrient solution to be added to the water that will be supplied to the plants. *Nutrient solutions will be explored in greater detail in Chapter 6.*

You will recall in the Chapter 1 discussion about the history of hydroponic gardening that John Woodward, in 1699, determined that pure water was not as good for soil-less plants when compared to water that once had soil soaked in it, which led to the important understanding of how water holds minerals once it has been in contact with soil. This discovery does not mean that plants are better off grown in soil, only that the minerals contained in the soil may be of use to the plants. Of course, minerals found in your backyard soil also may be bad for your plants or wholly negligible.

One of the best things about soil-less hydroponic gardening is that you have the power to be in complete control of the plant's nutrition. If you start with water that is completely neutral, you have to ability to give the plant only the nutrients that will help it grow while omitting any negative minerals and or chemicals that may be found in the soil. Your task is to learn what the best diet is for your garden.

Chapter 4

HYDROPONIC GARDENING SYSTEMS

hapter 1 provided a quick overview of a number of basic hydroponic gardening systems. Here, we will describe in greater detail how each of those systems works and how you can begin to design a system that is right for your particular situation. You will discover that many of the systems employ similar equipment. Chapter 7 will describe in greater detail the equipment that is essential to hydroponic gardening with some tips on where to get it and/or how to build it yourself.

Essentially, all hydroponic gardening systems do the same thing, as only a couple of tasks need to be accomplished for a successful hydroponic garden. The two primary functions of your system are to support the root system of the plants and to provide nutrients. There are many ways in which to accomplish these tasks. Each hydroponic gardening system described here employs a slightly different strategy for accomplishing these two vital functions.

You can build some of the simpler systems described here yourself, even if you have limited experience. Some of the more complex systems will require you to have a greater capability, but they are still within the realm of the experienced do-it-yourselfer.

As you explore each of the hydroponic gardening systems described here, you also will see that each system can be designed and built with varying levels of complexity. You will recall that systems were described in Chapter 1 as being static or dynamic. Some of the systems below can be designed and built as either static or dynamic, depending on how you deal with nutrient runoff.

The simplest and most basic hydroponic gardening systems must meet the two essential needs as mentioned above: root support and nutrient delivery. As such, your only requirement for such a basic system is a watertight container with some type of growing medium (growing media will be described in greater detail in Chapter 5) and a way in which to deliver a nutrient solution. The simpler the system, the easier these two tasks are to accomplish. For example, you might place a half-cup of lava stone in a quart yogurt container, drop a few basil seeds on the stones, and add water. This is as easy as it gets.

What you will find in your yogurt container hydroponic garden system as described above is that your basil seeds will probably sprout, and they may even take root. This will all happen within a few days, depending on the viability of the seeds. It is after these first few days that you will begin to have to answer:

- How much nutrient solution should be fed to the plant?
- How often should the plant be fed?
- In what manner should the nutrient solution be delivered to the plant?
- Does the system require air flow, as well as water?
- Should the system be drained in any way?
- Does it make a difference what material is used for growing media?

Each hydroponic gardening system answers these questions in a slightly different manner. You will discover also that different systems may work better for different types of plants.

In the end, the hydroponic gardening system(s) that you choose to start with and use should work well for you. That is, the system should be one that fits into your environment and lifestyle. Some hydroponic gardening systems have greater space and time demands than others. The goal of this chapter, and of this book, is to help you understand how each system works, and the space and time demands each system requires.

Note: If you read about each of these systems straight through, you will notice a good deal of repetition. You also should note the slight variations within the descriptions of each system, the system construction, and maintenance. The similarities and slight variations are very instructive.

The similarities are instructive as they show that each of these hydroponic gardening systems is based on the fundamental premise of the practice of hydroponic gardening. "Hydroponic gardening is a way of growing plants using water as the singular method of nutrient delivery."

The systems differ slightly in the manner in which each of them achieves this fundamental task. Each system has slightly different equipment that is put together and maintained in a slightly different manner.

This chapter is written so that you will learn how each of the systems described is related to each of the other systems, but also so that you can read about one system and understand how to construct and maintain the singular hydroponic gardening system.

Some of the systems detailed here allow seeds to be planted directly into the growing medium used in the system. Other systems will require you to germinate and prepare seeds before transplanting them into the system. Chapters 8 and 9 will instruct you as to the proper preparation of seeds for the hydroponic gardening system(s) of your choosing.

Static Hydroponic Gardening Systems

Raft systems

The raft system is a simple and easy-to-construct system. Because of this, it is a great system to experiment with, especially for the novice hydroponic gardener. You can construct a raft system that will accommodate a single plant or you can build a raft system for dozens of plants. You will recall the description in Chapter 1 of the "chinampas" of central Mexico. These floating gardens that were constructed by draining an area of a lake and built upon reeds that were woven over the lake bed before the area was flooded again. This is a good example of large raft hydroponic gardening system.

Raft systems are most commonly used with lettuce, herbs, and other small leafy plants. The reason for this is due to the lightweight nature of the plants. Growing plants that produce heavy fruit or vegetation might risk sinking a raft. Once you get a raft system up and running, you  can have a constant supply of fresh leafy greens because of the speed at which they will grow in a well-maintained raft hydroponic gardening system.

The basic premise of the raft system, like the chinampas of Mexico, is that the growing plants float on top of a reservoir of nutrient solution. The main parts are floating components to hold your plants on the surface of the solution, a large container to use as a reservoir, and a pump that will keep your nutrient solution well aerated because the water in the reservoir is not moving.

The raft system described here is about as simple a system as you can build. Essentially, your plants will be grown in small mesh pots that rest in a floating raft. The raft is made of a lightweight material such as Styrofoam that floats on the surface of a pool of water/nutrient solution in a tub or a shallow pan that serves as the reservoir. The plant's roots will grow through the mesh pots down into the nutrient solution in the reservoir. An air pump, similar to the type of pump used in fish aquariums, keeps the nutrient solution well aerated, delivering oxygen to the roots of the plants.

Materials you will need:

- Reservoir pan (A plastic storage bin that is about 23½" x 14½" x 6" deep on the inside works well. You can find these at most large retailers for $10 to $15. Try to find a bin that is opaque as opposed to a bin that is clear. If you can only find a clear storage bin, you will have to paint it or cover it in some fashion so sunlight does not get into the bin.)
- Styrofoam sheet (This needs to be a rigid piece of Styrofoam that is 1½" to 2" thick and large enough so you will be able to cut it down to fit inside the top of the reservoir.)
- Six 2" mesh cups
- Small bag of a lightweight expanded clay aggregate (You will find this at online retailers listed in the back of this book. This material is often listed as Leca®. This material is used as an anchor for the plant roots).
- Aquarium air pump
- Six feet of airline tubing (This tubing will run from the air pump into the reservoir.)
- "T" connector(s) (to connect the tubing to the pump and airstone)
- 5" airstone (Airstone is a porous stone, the type you find in fish aquariums, that will diffuse the air being sent

into the reservoir by the air pump. Airstone might be a natural material such as limewood or sandstone, but it also could be a man-made commercial product such as a Bubble Wand. These products cost about $5 to $10 and can be found at the online retailers found in the back of this book or at pet stores that deal in aquarium supplies.)

Tools you will need:

- Electric or battery-powered drill
- $3/8''$ or $1/2''$ chuck $1^7/8''$ hole saws for cutting plant sites
- Jigsaw or coping saw for cutting foam
- Razor knife for cutting tubing
- A pen or marker

Instructions:

- Measure the opening at the top of the reservoir container.
- Cut the Styrofoam so that it will fit into the top of the reservoir container. (You will want to cut it so that it will slide up and down a few inches into the container, but not have much more than $1/2''$ opening around the sides. The Styrofoam will act as a raft that floats on top of the water nutrient solution. The Styrofoam you cut should mimic the shape of the interior of the reservoir container you have chosen.)
- Mark six places where six holes will be cut through the Styrofoam. The spots marked should be equidistant from each other and the sides of the reservoir container.
- Cut six circular holes in the Styrofoam to accommodate the six mesh pots. (The pots should be able to fit snuggly into the Styrofoam and not fall through.)
- Place the airstone at the bottom of the reservoir.

- Connect the tubing to the pump and the airstone.
- Fill the reservoir with water/nutrient solution.
- Place the Styrofoam raft on top of the water/ nutrient solution.
- Place the mesh pots with the Leca (lightweight expanded clay aggregate) into the Styrofoam raft.

This is the basic system setup. The design is simple enough so that if you want to alter it in any way, you easily can use different materials to accomplish the same purpose. Example: rather than using a sheet of Styrofoam, you might consider alternative floating devices. If you would want to make individual rafts for each of the pots you could slice one-and-one-half to two-inch sections of a pool noodle and shape it into a ring in which to fit the mesh pots. You could link the rings together with monofilament fishing line and float them in the reservoir water/nutrient solution. To block sunlight from the reservoir you might employ a dark-colored piece of tarp or plastic such as a trash bag.

You might use many alternatives to the Leca (lightweight expanded clay aggregate). Chapter 5 will guide you through a variety of growing aggregates that you might use in your hydroponic raft system.

Once you get a basic system built, you may feel like experimenting with a wide variety of materials and products that suit your needs, wants, abilities, and environment. Do not be afraid to experiment.

Note that there has not been instruction here as to how to plant in the raft hydroponic garden. You will not plant seeds in the garden but, rather, plugs that have been started in another environment. Plugs are seeds that have developed from seeds and sprouts into shoots in a moss plug. *The starting of plugs will be discussed in Chapter 8.*

Once you have plugs started, you will place the plugs in the mesh cups and anchor each cup with the Leca. The mesh cups then will be placed in the holes cuts into the Styrofoam.

As the Styrofoam will be floating on the surface of the water/nutrient solution, the bottoms of the mesh cups will be submersed in the solution. Be sure when you place the cups in the raft that the roots of the plants are in contact with the water/nutrient solution.

Maintaining your hydroponic raft system:

Maintaining your hydroponic gardening system is important to protecting your plant's health (guarding against disease) and to clear the system of precipitates such as calcium and other minerals that may be in your water/nutrient solution.

How often you clean your entire system is entirely up to you. Some will maintain that you should cleanse your system after each harvest. This is a costly and time-consuming proposition.

It is not necessary for you clean your system after each crop is harvested. A good rule is to maintain records of how much water/nutrient solution you use to top off your system each time you have to add it to keep the levels up. Once you reach the point that you have added half the amount that the reservoir holds (Example: If your reservoir holds 34 gallons, your replacement amount would peak at 17 gallons of water/nutrient solution), you then would allow the water/nutrient solution to dissipate naturally to the point where you would need to top it off again and then prepare an entire new batch. At this point, you can clean the entire system.

It is vital that you keep a sharp eye on your system and the plants to determine if there is a problem related to cleanliness, bacteria, or algae. If so, it will be necessary to clean the system rather than wait until you have reached that 17-gallon limit.

After you have determined it is time to clean your system, dismantle the system by removing the plants, the mesh pots, and the Leca from the Styrofoam raft.

Remove the Styrofoam raft from the reservoir and discard the water/nutrient solution.

Clean all components with hot water and a good sanitizer such as Star San®.

Fill the reservoir with water and add household bleach at a level of four teaspoons per gallon of water.

Mix the bleach into the water and allow to soak for 24 to 72 hours.

While the system is soaking, run the pump in 15-minute cycles every hour to clean the hoses.

After the reservoir has soaked, discard the bleach solution and flush the whole system several times with fresh water to rid the system of the bleach and any other materials dislodged by the cleaning.

If you choose to use tap water to flush your system, be sure that you have allowed the water to sit for 24 hours before using the water to allow any chlorine in the water to dissipate.

If you notice a build-up of precipitates such as calcium on the sides of your reservoir or in your pump unit, you may need to do an acid flush if the system.

For an acid flush:

Add water and hydrochloric acid at the rate of ¾ teaspoon per gallon of water to the reservoir. Your goal is to achieve a pH of 2.

Allow the reservoir to soak for 24 to 72 hours.

While the system is soaking, run the pump for at least 15 minutes in every hour.

After the system is done soaking, neutralize the soak water flushing solution to pH 5 to 6 with soda ash before discarding it.

Flush the whole system several times with fresh water to rid the system of the acid solution and any other materials dislodged by the cleaning.

If you choose to use tap water to flush your system, be sure that you have allowed the water to sit for 24 hours before using the water to allow any chlorine in the water to dissipate.

If you choose to use tap water as the basis for your water/nutrient solution, draw the water and allow it to sit for 24 hours. This allows the chlorine to dissipate.

Allow the water/nutrient solution to rest for two hours after you mix the nutrients into the water before you check the pH level. You get a more accurate pH reading this way.

Keep a thermometer near your hydroponic gardening system to help maintain the temperature between 60 and 80 degrees. Adhesive thermometer strips that you apply directly to your reservoir are available. Alternatively, you can use an aquarium thermometer, but as it will be inside the reservoir, it will be difficult to read. If the water/nutrient solution gets too warm, you risk breeding bacteria that is bad for the plant's roots.

Put a small amount (a few drops) of hydrogen peroxide into your reservoir on a weekly basis. This will deter the growth of bacteria and algae.

Always check to make sure that the pump is running. If the pump stops, the water will become stagnant, and bacteria will start to grow. Also, the plant roots need the oxygen provided by the pump.

Always be sure that your pump is above the level of the reservoir so if your power goes out, there is no negative backflow into the pump.

Enclose the end of your pump hose in a screen to keep debris out of it.

Maintaining system cleanliness is vital to the health and well-being of your plants and your system. Keep a record of your cleaning. This will allow for greatest system efficiency.

The resource directory in the back of this book will direct you to supplies to help you maintain the cleanliness of your system and the health of your plants. Chapter 10 will go into greater detail related to ongoing maintenance issues of your hydroponic gardening system and your plants.

Bubbler System

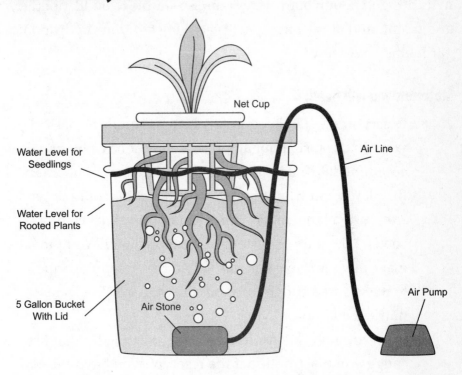

The bubbler system is another very easy-to-build hybrid hydroponic system that combines the elements of the previously described raft system and the bucket system that is described next. The difference between the raft system and this bubbler system is that the plants will not be floating in a raft on top of the water/nutrient solution but will be in a fixed position lid on top of the reservoir.

Because the plants will grow in a fixed lid on top of the reservoir, you can grow plants that might be somewhat heavier than the plants you could grow on the floating raft described above.

In many ways, this system is even more basic than the raft system in its design, though both systems are so simple to build, operate, and maintain that they are great places to start your hydroponic gardening adventure.

Materials you will need:

- Reservoir pan (To keep this system as simple as possible, you can use just about any reservoir that has a lid or can accommodate a lid and is big enough to accommodate the plants you want to grow. This reservoir could be as simple as a large mayonnaise jar, a plastic bucket, or a cooler. Like the raft system reservoir, you will want to make any reservoir you employ in this system opaque to make sure sunlight cannot penetrate into the water/ nutrient solution.)

- Reservoir lid (This needs to be a tight-fitting lid that fits snuggly in place on top if the reservoir you have chosen. Ideally, you have chosen a reservoir that has its own custom lid.)

- Cup(s) (The number of cups will be determined by the size of the reservoir and lid you are using. You can build this bubbler system with one cup, with six cups, or with a dozen cups, depending on the size reservoir and lid. Like the raft system, the cups can be mesh cups, or you simply can cut holes in some plastic cups.)

- Growing medium (You can use the lightweight expanded clay aggregate [Leca], as you did in the raft system, or you can try using some other medium such as rock wool or perlite. This material is used as an anchor for the plant roots).

- Aquarium air pump

- Six feet of airline tubing (This tubing will run from the air pump into the reservoir.)
- "T" connector(s) (to connect the tubing to the pump and airstone)
- 5" airstone (Airstone is a porous stone, the type you find in fish aquariums, that will diffuse the air that is being sent into the reservoir by the air pump. Airstone might be a natural material such as limewood or sandstone, but it could also be a man-made commercial product such as a Bubble Wand. These products cost about $5 to $10 and can be found at the online retailers found in the back of this book or at pet stores that deal in aquarium supplies.)

Tools you will need:
- Electric or battery-powered drill
- $3/8$" or $1/2$" chuck $1^7/8$" hole saws for cutting plant sites
- Jigsaw or coping saw for cutting holes in the reservoir lid
- Razor knife for cutting tubing
- A pen or marker

Instructions:
- Determine the number of plant cups you will have in the lid of your reservoir.
- Mark places where holes will be cut through the lid of the reservoir. The spots marked should be equidistant from each other and the sides of the reservoir container.
- Cut circular holes in the Styrofoam to accommodate the plant cups. (The pots should be able to fit snuggly into the Styrofoam and not fall through.)
- If there is a tight-fitting reservoir lid, you also may need to cut a small hole to accommodate the air pump tubing.

- Place the airstone at the bottom of the reservoir.
- Connect the tubing to the pump and the airstone
- Fill the reservoir with water/nutrient solution.
- Place the lid on top of the reservoir filled with water/ nutrient solution.
- Place the plant cups with the Leca (lightweight expanded clay aggregate) into the lid of the reservoir, making sure that the bottoms of the cups come in contact with the water/nutrient solution.

This is the basic system setup. The design is simple enough so that if you want to alter it in any way, you can easily use different materials to accomplish the same purpose.

Once you get a basic system built, you may feel like experimenting with a wide variety of materials and products that suit your needs, wants, abilities and environment. Do not be afraid to experiment.

Note that there has not been instruction here as to how to plant in the bubbler hydroponic garden. You will not plant seeds in the garden but, rather, plugs that have been started in another environment. Plugs are seeds that have developed from seeds and sprouts into shoots in a moss plug. The starting of plugs will be discussed in Chapter 8.

Once you have plugs started, you will place the plugs in the mesh cups and anchor each cup with the Leca. The mesh cups then will be placed in the holes cuts into the lid of the reservoir.

Maintaining your hydroponic bubbler system:

Maintaining your hydroponic gardening system is important to protecting your plant's health (guarding against disease) and to clear the system of precipitates such as calcium and other minerals that may be in your water/nutrient solution.

How often you clean your entire system is entirely up to you. Some will maintain that you should cleanse your system after each harvest. This is a costly and time-consuming proposition.

It is not necessary for you clean your system after each crop is harvested. A good rule is to maintain records of how much water/nutrient solution you use to top off your system each time you have to add it to keep the levels up. Once you reach the point that you have added half the amount that the reservoir holds (Example: If your reservoir holds 34 gallons, your replacement amount would peak at 17 gallons of water/nutrient solution), you then would allow the water/nutrient solution to dissipate naturally to the point where you would need to top it off again and then prepare an entire new batch. At this point, you can clean the entire system.

It is vital that you keep a sharp eye on your system and the plants to determine if there is a problem related to cleanliness, bacteria, or algae. If so, it will be necessary to clean the system rather than wait until you have reached that 17-gallon limit.

After you have determined it is time to clean your system, dismantle the system by removing the plants, the plant cups, and the Leca from the reservoir lid.

Remove the reservoir lid from the reservoir and discard the water/nutrient solution.

Clean all components with hot water and a good sanitizer such as Star San.

Fill the reservoir with water and add household bleach at a level of four teaspoons per gallon of water.

Mix the bleach into the water and allow to soak for 24 to 72 hours.

While the system is soaking, run the pump in 15-minute cycles every hour to clean the hoses.

After the reservoir has soaked, discard the bleach solution and flush the whole system several times with fresh water to rid the system of the bleach and any other materials dislodged by the cleaning.

If you choose to use tap water to flush your system, be sure that you have allowed the water to sit for 24 hours before using the water to allow any chlorine in the water to dissipate.

If you notice a build-up of precipitates such as calcium on the sides of your reservoir or in your pump unit, you may need to do an acid flush if the system.

For an acid flush:

Add water and hydrochloric acid at the rate of ¾ teaspoon per gallon of water to the reservoir. Your goal is to achieve a pH of 2.

Allow the reservoir to soak for 24 to 72 hours.

While the system is soaking, run the pump for at least 15 minutes in every hour.

After the system is done soaking, neutralize the soak water flushing solution to pH 5 to 6 with soda ash before discarding it.

Flush the whole system several times with fresh water to rid the system of the acid solution and any other materials dislodged by the cleaning.

If you choose to use tap water to flush your system, be sure that you have allowed the water to sit for 24 hours before using the water to allow any chlorine in the water to dissipate.

If you choose to use tap water as the basis for your water/nutrient solution, draw the water and allow it to sit for 24 hours. This allows the chlorine to dissipate.

Allow the water/nutrient solution to rest for two hours after you mix the nutrients into the water before you check the pH level. You get a more accurate pH reading this way

Keep a thermometer near your hydroponic gardening system to help maintain the temperature between 60 and 80 degrees. Adhesive thermometer strips that you apply directly to your reservoir are available. Alternatively, you can use an aquarium thermometer, but as it will be inside the reservoir, it will be difficult to read. If the water/nutrient solution gets too warm, you risk breeding bacteria that is bad for the plant's roots.

Put a small amount (a few drops) of hydrogen peroxide into your reservoir on a weekly basis. This will deter the growth of bacteria and algae.

Always check to make sure that the pump is running. If the pump stops, the water will become stagnant, and bacteria will start to grow. Also, the plant roots need the oxygen provided by the pump.

Always be sure that your pump is above the level of the reservoir so if your power goes out, there is no negative backflow into the pump. Enclose the end of your pump hose in a screen to keep debris out of it.

Maintaining system cleanliness is vital to the health and well-being of your plants and your system. Keep a record of your cleaning. This will allow for greatest system efficiency.

The resource directory in the back of this book will direct you to supplies to help you maintain the cleanliness of your system and the health of your plants. Chapter 10 will go into greater detail related to ongoing maintenance issues of your hydroponic gardening system and your plants.

Bucket Systems

This is sometimes called a deep water culture because it has a much deeper reservoir of water than some of the other types. Each bucket needs a support for the plant, which is usually a net basket for growing medium attached to the underside lid of the reservoir and a bubbler. Alternatively, we also will detail a bucket system in which you can grow your plant in growing medium placed directly in the bucket. A bucket system can be very basic, often using off-the-shelf Rubbermaid totes as the main reservoir. This is another good place to start if you plan on going the DIY route, much like the bubbler and raft systems.

Several permutations of the bucket system will be detailed here. One of the systems requires no pumps and the plants are grown directly in the growing medium without the need for pots. The other systems are much like the bubbler described earlier and use an oxygenating pump. The more advanced bucket system is also a bridge to a system that will be described later on in this chapter called the top-drip system.

The roots grow through the medium and mesh basket directly into the pool of liquid below in the reservoir. The solution already is aerated due to the bubbler, and the top portion of the roots is suspended above the liquid for additional breathing space.

The "no-pump" bucket

This is another system type that can make the claim, "It does not get any simpler than this." This system uses the fewest number of materials than any system described in this book and is very easy to construct, use, and maintain.

Materials you will need:

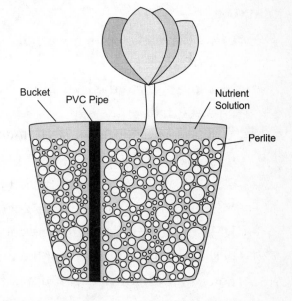

- Five-gallon plastic bucket made of food-grade plastic (Food-grade plastic is plastic deemed safe for use by the Food and Drug Administration. The bucket should be opaque. If the bucket is a light color or clear, you should paint the bucket a dark color.).

- ½" diameter PVC pipe that is as long as the bucket is tall
- Enough growing medium to fill the bucket to within 1" of the top of the bucket (The preferred growing medium for this system is perlite. Perlite is a lightweight volcanic glass that has high water content. It is a common growing medium for hydroponic gardening systems. The perlite to fill a five-gallon bucket will cost about $15. It is available at many large hardware stores or garden centers.)
- A wooden dowel rod slightly longer than the PVC pipe.

Tool you will need:

Saw

Instructions:

- Clean the bucket with household bleach or some other sanitizing agent.
- Measure and cut the PVC pipe so it is as long as the bucket is tall.
- Measure and cut the wooden dowel rod so it is about three inches longer than the PVC pipe.
- Stand the PVC pipe in the bucket (anywhere away from the very edge of the bucket is good).
- Hold the PVC pipe upright as you fill the bucket with the perlite to within one inch of the top of the bucket.
- Pour a water/nutrient solution into the perlite filled bucket to within two to three inches of the top fill of perlite.

- Use the dowel rod to check the level of water/nutrient solution by inserting the dowel rod into the PVC pipe. The dowel rod and PVC pipe with act like the dipstick that checks the oil in your car. The level of the water/ nutrient solution will be seen on the dowel rod.

The "no-pump" bucket system is now ready to be used. You can plant seeds directly into the perlite, or you can choose to transplant seeds that have been germinated elsewhere into the perlite.

This system does not employ a pump because the roots of the plant will get oxygen from the several inches of space left between the top of the perlite and the top of the level of water/ nutrient solution. As the roots of the plant grow, you can decrease the level of water/nutrient solution from two inches to as much as ten inches. Continue to use the dowel rod to check the level of the water/nutrient solution.

The upper level of perlite not submersed in the water/nutrient solution will provide the plant roots with the necessary oxygen.

Refer to Chapter 6 for more on water/nutrient solutions.

Maintaining your hydroponic "no-pump" bucket system:

Maintaining your hydroponic gardening system is important to protecting your plant's health (guarding against disease) and to clear the system of precipitates such as calcium and other minerals that may be in your water/nutrient solution.

How often you clean your entire system is entirely up to you. Some will maintain that you should cleanse your system after each harvest. This is a costly and time-consuming proposition.

It is not necessary for you clean your system after each crop is harvested. A good rule is to maintain records of how much water/nutrient solution you use to top off your system each time you have to add it to keep the levels up. Once you reach the point that you have added half the amount that the reservoir holds (Example: If you add four gallons to your bucket, your replacement amount would peak at two gallons of water/nutrient solution), you then would allow the water/nutrient solution to dissipate naturally to the point where you would need to top it off again and then prepare a new batch. At this point, you can clean the entire system.

It is vital that you keep a sharp eye on your system and the plants to determine if there is a problem related to the cleanliness, bacteria, or algae. If so, it will be necessary to clean the system rather than wait until you have reached that two-gallon limit.

After you have determined it is time to clean your system, dismantle the system by removing the plants, the plant cups, and the perlite from the bucket.

Discard the water/nutrient solution.

It is possible to clean and reuse the perlite by soaking it in a weak bleach/water solution and then allowing it to dry. You can dry it by spreading it out in a thin layer on a large drop cloth. That said, perlite is very inexpensive, and you may just choose to dispose of it and use a new bag.

Clean all components with hot water and a good sanitizer such as Star San.

Fill the bucket with water and add household bleach at a level of four teaspoons per gallon of water.

Mix the bleach into the water and allow to soak for 24 to 72 hours.

After the bucket has soaked, discard the bleach solution and rinse the bucket several times with fresh water to rid the bucket of the bleach and any other materials dislodged by the cleaning.

If you choose to use tap water to rinse your bucket, be sure that you have allowed the water to sit for 24 hours before using the water to allow any chlorine in the water to dissipate.

If you notice a build-up of precipitates such as calcium on the sides of your bucket, you may need to do an acid wash of the bucket.

For an acid wash:

Add water and hydrochloric acid at the rate of ¾ teaspoon per gallon of water to the bucket. Your goal is to achieve a pH of 2.

If there is a precipitate on the PVC pipe, place the PVC into the acid wash in the bucket.

Allow the bucket and PVC pipe to soak for 24 to 72 hours.

After the components are done soaking, neutralize the soak water flushing solution to pH 5 to 6 with soda ash before discarding it.

Rinse the components several times with fresh water to rid them of the acid solution and any other materials dislodged by the cleaning.

If you choose to use tap water to flush your system, be sure that you have allowed the water to sit for 24 hours before using the water to allow any chlorine in the water to dissipate.

If you choose to use tap water as the basis for your water/nutrient solution, draw the water and allow it to sit for 24 hours. This allows the chlorine to dissipate.

Allow the water/nutrient solution to rest for two hours after you mix the nutrients into the water before you check the pH level. You get a more accurate pH reading this way.

Keep a thermometer near your hydroponic gardening system to help maintain the temperature between 60 and 80 degrees. Adhesive thermometer strips that you apply directly to your bucket are available. If the water/nutrient solution gets too warm, you risk breeding bacteria that is bad for the plant's roots.

Put a small amount (a few drops) of hydrogen peroxide into your bucket on a weekly basis. This will deter the growth of bacteria and algae.

Maintaining system cleanliness is vital to the health and well-being of your plants and your system. Keep a record of cleaning. This will allow for greatest system efficiency.

The resource directory in the back of this book will direct you to supplies to help you maintain the cleanliness of your system and the health of your plants. Chapter 10 will go into greater detail related to ongoing maintenance issues of your hydroponic gardening system and your plants.

Bubbler bucket system

If you have already read and/or constructed a simple bubbler system, you will recognize the design and be familiar with the construction of this bubbler bucket hydroponic gardening system. The system is described in detail here, as it will lead you to further exploration of the many permutations of bucket system hydroponic gardening.

If you have not yet seen how each of these systems employ very similar characteristics, this bubbler bucket system and the systems that follow will show you that the fundamentals of hydroponic gardening are very basic and that most hydroponic garden-

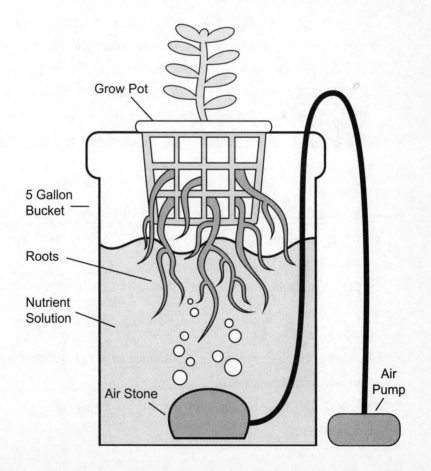

ing systems adhere to the simple action of delivering a water/ nutrient solution to plants in a soil-less environment.

The bubbler bucket described here is for a singular plant. This system is good for larger plants such as tomatoes, tomatillos, or peppers. Later in this chapter you will learn how to link these pots together in a larger singular system.

Materials you will need:

- A five-gallon size bucket with lid (You will want to make any bucket you employ in this system opaque to make sure sunlight cannot penetrate into the water/ nutrient solution.)
- 6" diameter mesh pot with a rim (The openings in the mesh pot should be able to accommodate the growth of roots through the mesh. A fine mesh will not work for this. The openings in the mesh should be ¼". Since you will be filling the pot with a growing medium, there is not too much concern about the mesh being too large, as long as the growing medium remains in the pot when it is filled.)
- Growing medium (You can use the lightweight expanded clay aggregate [Leca], as you did in the raft system, or you can try using some other medium such as rock wool or perlite. This material is used as an anchor for the plant roots).
- Aquarium air pump
- Six feet of airline tubing (This tubing will run from the air pump into the reservoir.)
- "T" connector(s) (to connect the tubing to the pump and airstone)

- 5" airstone (Airstone is a porous stone, the type you find in fish aquariums, that will diffuse the air that is being sent into the reservoir by the air pump. Airstone might be a natural material such as limewood or sandstone, but it could also be a man-made commercial product such as a Bubble Wand. These products cost about $5 to $10 and can be found at the online retailers found in the back of this book or at pet stores that deal in aquarium supplies.)

Tools you will need:

- Jigsaw or coping saw for cutting hole in the bucket lid
- Drill with ¼" drill bit
- Razor knife for cutting tubing
- A pen or marker

Instructions:

- Determine the size of mesh pot you will have in the lid of your bucket.
- Mark place where hole will be cut through the lid of the bucket. You can trace the top of the pot on the bucket lid and then make a slightly smaller hole so the pot can be inserted into the lid without falling through into the bucket.
- Cut a circular hole in the bucket lid to accommodate the plant pot. (The pot should be able to fit snuggly into the lid and not fall through.)
- Using the drill with the ¼" drill bit, drill a small hole to accommodate the air pump tubing.
- Place the airstone at the bottom of the bucket.
- Connect the tubing to the pump and the airstone.
- Fill the bucket with water/nutrient solution.

- Place the lid on top of the bucket filled with water/ nutrient solution.
- Place the plant pot with the Leca (lightweight expanded clay aggregate) into the lid of the bucket, making sure that the bottom of the pot comes into contact with the water/nutrient solution.

This is the basic system setup. The design is simple enough so that if you want to alter it in any way, you easily can use different materials to accomplish the same purpose. The system will be expanded upon later in this chapter.

Once you get a basic system built, you may feel like experimenting with a wide variety of materials and products that suit your needs, wants, abilities and environment. Do not be afraid to experiment.

Note that there has not been instruction here as to how to plant in the bubbler bucket hydroponic system. You will not plant seeds in the garden but, rather, plugs that have been started in another environment. Plugs are seeds that have developed from seeds and sprouts into shoots in a moss plug. The starting of plugs will be discussed in Chapter 10.

Once you have plugs started, you will place the plugs in the plant pot and anchor the pot with the Leca. The mesh pot will then be placed in the hole cut into the lid of the bucket.

Maintaining your bubbler bucket system:

Maintaining your hydroponic gardening system is important to protecting your plant's health (guarding against disease) and to clear the system of precipitates such as calcium and other minerals that may be in your water/nutrient solution.

How often you clean your entire system is entirely up to you. Some will maintain that you should cleanse your system after each harvest. This is a costly and time-consuming proposition.

It is not necessary for you clean your system after each crop is harvested. A good rule is to maintain records of how much water/nutrient solution you use to top off your system each time you have to add it to keep the levels up. Once you reach the point that you have added half the amount that the reservoir holds (Example: If your bucket holds four gallons, your replacement amount would peak at two gallons of water/nutrient solution), you then would allow the water/nutrient solution to dissipate naturally to the point where you would need to top it off again and then prepare an entire new batch. At this point, you can clean the entire system.

It is vital that you keep a sharp eye on your system and the plants to determine if there is a problem related to the cleanliness, bacteria, or algae. If so, it will be necessary to clean the system rather than wait until you have reached that two-gallon limit.

After you have determined it is time to clean your system, dismantle the system by removing the plants, the plant pot, and the Leca from the bucket lid.

Remove the bucket lid from the bucket and discard the water/nutrient solution.

Clean all components with hot water and a good sanitizer such as Star San.

Fill the bucket with water and add household bleach at a level of four teaspoons per gallon of water.

Mix the bleach into the water and allow to soak for 24 to 72 hours.

While the system is soaking, run the pump in 15-minute cycles every hour to clean the hoses.

After the bucket has soaked, discard the bleach solution and flush the whole system several times with fresh water to rid the system of the bleach and any other materials dislodged by the cleaning.

If you choose to use tap water to flush your system, be sure that you have allowed the water to sit for 24 hours before using the water to allow any chlorine in the water to dissipate.

If you notice a build-up of precipitates such as calcium on the sides of your bucket or in your pump unit, you may need to do an acid flush if the system.

For an acid flush:

Add water and hydrochloric acid at the rate of ¾ teaspoon per gallon of water to the bucket. Your goal is to achieve a pH of 2.

Allow the bucket to soak for 24 to 72 hours.

While the system is soaking, run the pump at least 15 minutes in every hour.

After the system is done soaking, neutralize the soak water flushing solution to pH 5 to 6 with soda ash before discarding it.

Flush the whole system several times with fresh water to rid the system of the acid solution and any other materials dislodged by the cleaning.

If you choose to use tap water to flush your system, be sure that you have allowed the water to sit for 24 hours before using the water to allow any chlorine in the water to dissipate.

If you choose to use tap water as the basis for your water/nutrient solution, draw the water and allow it to sit for 24 hours. This allows the chlorine to dissipate.

Allow the water/nutrient solution to rest for two hours after you mix the nutrients into the water before you check the pH level. You get a more accurate pH reading this way

Keep a thermometer near your hydroponic gardening system to help maintain the temperature between 60 and 80 degrees. Adhesive thermometer strips that you apply directly to your bucket are available. Alternatively, you can use an aquarium thermometer, but as it will be inside the bucket, it will be difficult to read. If the water/nutrient solution gets too warm, you risk breeding bacteria that is bad for the plant's roots.

Put a small amount (a few drops) of hydrogen peroxide into your bucket on a weekly basis. This will deter the growth of bacteria and algae.

Always check to make sure that the pump is running. If the pump stops, the water will become stagnant and bacteria will start to grow. Also, the plant roots need the oxygen provided by the pump.

Always be sure that your pump is above the level of the bucket. This is so that if your power goes out, there is no negative backflow into the pump.

Enclose the end of your pump hose in a screen to keep debris out of it.

Maintaining system cleanliness is vital to the health and well-being of your plants and your system. Keep a record of your cleaning. This will allow for greatest system efficiency.

The resource directory in the back of this book will direct you to supplies to help you maintain the cleanliness of your system and the health of your plants. Chapter 10 will go into greater detail related to ongoing maintenance issues of your hydroponic gardening system and your plants.

Wick Systems

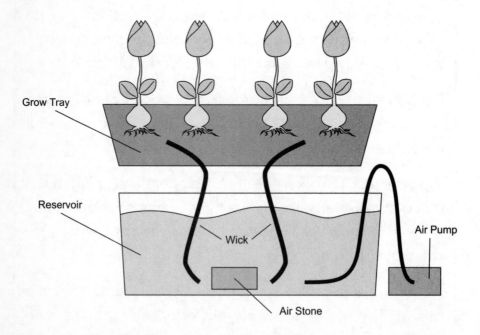

You will recall that the primary focus of all gardening systems is the delivery of nutrients to the plants. Soil-based gardening, aeroponic gardening, and hydroponic gardening all have this one strategy in common.

Wick systems are really one of the simplest type of hydroponic gardening systems, as they may be made without pumps or any moving parts at all. Nutrient solution is drawn up from a small reservoir under your plants into the main pot with the growing medium. Cloth strips or even short lengths of cotton rope are used as the wicks. Alternatively, the medium itself can be in contact with the water, and it will naturally absorb on its own. This approach will lead to wetter medium compared to the use of actual wicks.

This method is more like conventional "dirt gardening" because the plants roots usually are held completely within the mass of growing medium rather than exposed to the nutrient solution directly. The medium that you use for these types of arrangements must be absorbent (vermiculite, coco fibre, or moss) but also will need to have enough drainage throughout to allow some air. The medium will stay wet constantly and can drown the roots otherwise.

The main benefit of using a wick system is the simplicity and the independence from a power source. Unlike the other options, this one will continue working just fine even if there is a prolonged power outage. Nutrient solution is not reclaimed or recycled through the system. You just have to refill the reservoir when the volume gets low.

A lack of air content for the roots makes this a less adequate choice for many plants though. Adding a bubbler to the reservoir can help, but once the water has soaked up through the wicks and the medium, most air content will be gone.

Materials you will need:

- Reservoir pan (To keep this system as simple as possible, you can use just about any reservoir that has a lid or can accommodate a lid and is big enough to accommodate the plants you want to grow. The ideal reservoir might be a plastic storage tote with a lid, though this reservoir could be as simple as a large mayonnaise jar, a plastic bucket, or a cooler. You will need to be able to place the plant pan on top of the reservoir. Like the raft system reservoir, you will want to make any reservoir you employ in this system opaque to make sure sunlight cannot penetrate into the water/nutrient solution.)
- Reservoir lid (This needs to be a tight-fitting lid that fits snuggly in place on top if the reservoir you have chosen. Ideally, you have chosen a reservoir that has its own custom lid.)
- Plant pan (Ideally, the plant pan should be similar in size to the reservoir pan. The plant pan will sit on top of the reservoir. Thus, if the two containers are of a similar size and manufactured as stackable units, the construction of this wick system is made easier.)
- Plant pan lid (Like the reservoir lid, this needs to be a tight-fitting lid that fits snuggly in place on top if the plant pan you have chosen. Ideally, you have chosen a plant pan that has its own custom lid.)
- Cup(s) (The number of cups will be determined by the size of the reservoir and lid you are using. You can build this bubbler system with one cup, six cups, or with a

dozen cups, depending on the size reservoir and lid. Like the raft system, the cups can be mesh cups, or you simply can cut holes in some plastic cups.)

- Growing medium (The lightweight expanded clay aggregate [Leca] you may have used in the raft system is not the ideal medium for the wick system. You will want to use a medium that has wicking ability, such as rock wool or perlite. A combination of materials such as vermiculite, perlite, and coconut coir also would be a good choice. This material is used as an anchor for the plant roots).

- Six to eight feet of absorbent rope (The rope is used as the wick to move the water/nutrient solution from the reservoir to the plant pan. The rope you choose could be nylon, cotton, or rope made of any other absorbent material. Test the absorption quality of the rope before you use it by placing one end of it in water. After an hour, you will see how much water has been soaked to the end of the rope out of the water. If the rope is only a little wet, try washing the rope in a washing machine and testing it again.)

- Aquarium air pump

- Six feet of airline tubing (This tubing will run from the air pump into the reservoir.)

- "T" connector(s) (to connect the tubing to the pump and airstone)

- 5" airstone (Airstone is a porous stone, the type you find in fish aquariums, that will diffuse the air that is being sent into the reservoir by the air pump. Airstone might be a natural material such as limewood or sandstone, but it could also be a man-made commercial product such as a Bubble Wand. These products cost about $5 to $10 and can be found at the online retailers found in the back of this book or at pet stores that deal in aquarium supplies.)

Tools you will need:

- Electric or battery-powered drill
- ³/₈" or ½" chuck 1⁷/₈" hole saws for cutting plant sites
- Jigsaw or coping saw for cutting holes in the reservoir lid
- Razor knife for cutting tubing and rope
- A pen or marker

Instructions:

(These instructions are for a wick hydroponic gardening system constructed from two 18" x 23" x 21" [W x H x D] or approximately 17-gallon totes. One tote will be the reservoir and one will be the plant pan.)

- Mark six places where six holes will be cut through the lid of the top of the plant pan tote. The spots marked should be equidistant from each other and the sides of the plant pan tote.
- Cut six circular holes in the top of the plant pan tote to accommodate the six mesh pots. (The pots should be able to fit snuggly into the lid and not fall through.)
- Drill ½" holes in the bottom of the plant pan beneath the spots where the mesh pots will be placed. (These holes will accommodate the rope wicks.)
- Drill ½" holes in the lid of the water nutrient reservoir lid at the spots where the holes you have drilled in plant pan are situated when the plant pan is set on top of the

water/nutrient reservoir. (This will also accommodate the passage of the rope wicks.)

- Drill ½" hole in the side edge of the lid of the water/ nutrient reservoir lid to accommodate the tubing from the air pump.
- Place the airstone at the bottom of the reservoir.
- Connect the tubing to the pump and the airstone.
- Fill the reservoir with water/nutrient solution.
- Fill the plant pan tote with a 50/50 mixture of perlite/vermiculite.
- Run six rope wicks down through the 50/50 mixture of perlite/vermiculite, the holes in the bottom of the plant pan (the ropes should reach up to where your plants will be and be able to extend down into the water/ nutrient solution).
- Place the lid on top of the plant pan.
- Place the mesh pots filled with the growing medium in the holes in the lid of the plant pan.
- Fill the reservoir with water/nutrient solution.
- Place the lid on the reservoir with the water/ nutrient solution.
- Feed the rope wicks through the holes you have drilled in the lid of the reservoir filled with water/ nutrient solution.

This is the basic system setup. The design is simple enough so that if you want to alter it in any way, you can easily use different materials to accomplish the same purpose. Example: rather than using a sheet of Styrofoam, you might consider alternative floating devices. If you would want to make individual rafts for each of the pots you could slice one-and-one-half to two-inch sections of a pool noodle and shape it into a ring in which to fit the mesh pots. You could link the rings together with monofilament fishing line and float them in the reservoir water/nutrient solution. To block sunlight from the reservoir you might employ a dark-colored piece of tarp or plastic such as a trash bag.

You might use many alternatives to the Leca (lightweight expanded clay aggregate). Chapter 5 will guide you through a variety of growing aggregates that you might use in your hydroponic raft system.

Once you get a basic system built, you may feel like experimenting with a wide variety of materials and products that suit your needs, wants, abilities, and environment. Do not be afraid to experiment.

Maintaining your hydroponic wick system:

Maintaining your hydroponic gardening system is important to protecting your plant's health (guarding against disease) and to clear the system of precipitates such as calcium and other minerals that may be in your water/nutrient solution.

How often you clean your entire system is entirely up to you. Some will maintain that you should cleanse your system after each harvest. This is a costly and time-consuming proposition.

It is not necessary for you clean your system after each crop is harvested. A good rule is to maintain records of how much water/nutrient solution you use to top off your system each time you have to add it to keep the levels up. Once you reach the point that you have added half the amount that the reservoir holds (example: if your reservoir holds 34 gallons, your replacement amount would peak at 17 gallons of water/nutrient solution), you then would allow the water/nutrient solution to dissipate naturally to the point where you would need to top it off again and then prepare a new batch. At this point, you can clean the entire system.

It is vital that you keep a sharp eye on your system and the plants to determine if there is a problem related to cleanliness, bacteria, or algae. If so, it will be necessary to clean the system rather than wait until you have reached that 17-gallon limit.

After you have determined it is time to clean your system, dismantle the system by removing the plants, the mesh pots, and the growing medium.

Discard the water/nutrient solution.

Discard the wick rope.

Clean all components with hot water and a good sanitizer such as Star San.

Fill the reservoir and the plant pan with water and add household bleach at a level of four teaspoons per gallon of water.

Mix the bleach into the water and allow to soak for 24 to 72 hours.

While the system is soaking, run the pump in 15-minute cycles every hour to clean the hoses.

After the reservoir and plant pan have soaked, discard the bleach solution and flush the whole system several times with fresh water to rid the system of the bleach and any other materials dislodged by the cleaning.

If you choose to use tap water to flush your system, be sure that you have allowed the water to sit for 24 hours before using the water to allow any chlorine in the water to dissipate.

If you notice a build-up of precipitates such as calcium on the sides of your reservoir or in your pump unit, you may need to do an acid flush if the system.

For an acid flush:

Add water and hydrochloric acid at the rate of ¾ teaspoon per gallon of water to the reservoir. Your goal is to achieve a pH of 2.

Allow the reservoir to soak for 24 to 72 hours.

While the system is soaking, run the pump at least 15 minutes in every hour.

After the system is done soaking, neutralize the soak water flushing solution to pH 5 to 6 with soda ash before discarding it.

Flush the whole system several times with fresh water to rid the system of the acid solution and any other materials dislodged by the cleaning.

If you choose to use tap water to flush your system, be sure that you have allowed the water to sit for 24 hours before using the water to allow any chlorine in the water to dissipate.

If you choose to use tap water as the basis for your water/nutrient solution, draw the water and allow it to sit for 24 hours. This allows the chlorine to dissipate.

Allow the water/nutrient solution to rest for two hours after you mix the nutrients into the water before you check the pH level. You get a more accurate pH reading this way

Keep a thermometer near your hydroponic gardening system to help maintain the temperature between 60 and 80 degrees. Adhesive thermometer strips that you apply directly to you reservoir are available. Alternatively, you can use an aquarium thermometer, but as it will be inside the reservoir, it will be difficult to read. If the water/nutrient solution gets too warm, you risk breeding bacteria that is bad for the plant's roots.

Put a small amount (a few drops) of hydrogen peroxide into your reservoir on a weekly basis. This will deter the growth of bacteria and algae.

Always check to make sure that the pump is running. If the pump stops, the water will become stagnant and bacteria will start to grow. Also, the plant roots need the oxygen provided by the pump.

Always be sure that your pump is above the level of the reservoir so if your power goes out, there is no negative backflow into the pump.

Enclose the end of your pump hose in a screen to keep debris out of it.

Maintaining system cleanliness is vital to the health and well-being of your plants and your system. Keep a record of your cleaning. This will allow for greatest system efficiency.

The resource directory in the back of this book will direct you to supplies to help you maintain the cleanliness of your system and the health of your plants. Chapter 10 will go into greater detail related to ongoing maintenance issues of your hydroponic gardening system and your plants.

Dynamic Hydroponic Growing Systems

Top-drip bucket system

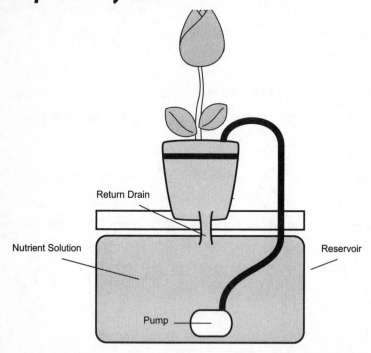

Just as you discovered the transformation of the basic sprout jar to the fundamental static systems of hydroponic gardening, you now will see how the systems will begin to grow in complexity as the static bucket system becomes a more dynamic top-drip bucket system. The bucket system detailed here differs from the earlier versions in that the nutrient is fed to the plant from a drip line at the top of the system. The system is considered a dynamic system because the nutrient flows through the system, drains at the bottom, and is collected for redistribution through the system. You also will see here that several buckets are linked to one feeder bucket that contains the water/nutrient solution.

This is not strictly a static system, since the water is moving, but it is closer to this style than any of the others. With a top drip, water is pumped from the bottom of the reservoir to above the plant support and growing medium. It then trickles down through the roots back to the reservoir. It is a continual loop. Bubblers are not needed because the constant motion of the water allows for natural aeration to take place, and the water will not stagnate.

Aside from the top/bottom bucket arrangement, you also will need a pump with hosing to move the water from the bottom to the top. This is a very common type of hydroponic system, and it can be expanded to work with large trays of plants rather than just a single bucket. Hoses also can connect several buckets and a central reservoir with a single large pump.

Materials you will need:

- Two five-gallon buckets with lids (As this system can be constructed to accommodate multiple grow pots, you can use as many buckets as you desire. The idea here is that one bucket contains the water/nutrient solution, and the other bucket contains the plant. Usually, there is one plant per bucket in a system with multiple grow pots.

You will want to make any bucket you employ in this system opaque to make sure sunlight cannot penetrate into the water/nutrient solution.)

- Two plastic or nylon marine thru-hull fittings (These pieces will fit into the drain holes drilled at the bottom of each bucket. The best fittings for a tight fit feature a nut that secures the fitting from the inside of the bucket. Drain and feeder tubing will be attached to the fittings.

- Four rubber gaskets (for the inside and outside of each bucket where the marine thru-hull fittings are placed.)

- 6" diameter mesh pot with a rim (The openings in the mesh pot should be able to accommodate the growth of roots through the mesh. A fine mesh will not work for this. The openings in the mesh should be ¼". Since you will be filling the pot with a growing medium, there is not too much of a concern about the mesh being too large as long as the growing medium remains in the pot when it is filled.)

- Small submersible pump (The pump needed here is one you might find in a garden pond. An example of such a pump is Little Giant PE-A that pumps at 80 gallons/hour or a PES-A that pumps at 63 gallons/hour. Pumps such as these sell for $45 to $60 at garden shops or online retailers.)

- Aquarium air pump
- Ten feet of airline tubing
- "T" connector
- 5" airstone
- PVC cement (4 oz. can should be enough)

- Aquarium grade silicone sealant (A small tube of this should be enough. You can buy this at any pet or aquarium shop.)
- Six feet ½" diameter black irrigation tubing
- Six feet ¼" irrigation "spaghetti" tubing (This will be your drip line.)

Tools you will need:

- Jigsaw or coping saw for cutting hole in the bucket lid
- Drill with ³/₄" drill bit and ¼" drill bit
- Razor knife for cutting tubing
- A pen or marker

Instructions:

- Cut holes about one to two inches above the bottom of each of the buckets. (It is a good idea to use black buckets, as they do not allow light to penetrate. These holes should be ³/₄" or the proper size to match the size of the marine thru-hull fittings you use.)
- Insert marine thru-hull fittings into each of the drilled holes.
- A rubber gasket and/or washer is then tightened on each side or on one side of the marine thru-hull fitting to tightly seal the drilled hole.
- Determine the size of mesh pot you will have in the lid of your bucket.
- Mark place where hole will be cut through the lid of the bucket. You can trace the top of the pot on the bucket lid and then make a slightly smaller hole so that the pot can be inserted into the lid without falling through into the bucket.

- Cut a circular hole in the bucket lid to accommodate the plant pot. (The pot should be able to fit snuggly into the lid and not fall through.)
- Place small submersible pump at the bottom of the bucket that will be your water/nutrient solution reservoir.
- Run length of ¼" irrigation "spaghetti" tubing spaghetti from pump to top of plant bucket.
- Connect length of ½" diameter black irrigation tubing from drain at bottom of plant bucket to intake marine thru-hull fitting and bottom of water/nutrient solution bucket.
- Fill the bucket with the pump in it with water/nutrient solution.
- Using the drill with the ¼" drill bit, drill a small hole to accommodate the air pump tubing.
- Place the lid on top of the bucket filled with water/ nutrient solution.
- Place the plant pot with the Leca (lightweight expanded clay aggregate) into the lid of the bucket.

This is the basic setup of the top-drip bucket system. Bucket systems often use configurations of multiple buckets for growing and one bucket to act as a reservoir for the returning water/nutrient solution. Gravity aids the water/nutrient solution in filtering through the growing medium to the bottom. Gravity also allows the runoff to return to the reservoir bucket.

Further on in this chapter, we will detail ways in which you can link multiple buckets together to expand your drip systems in a variety of configurations.

Maintaining your top-drip bucket system

Maintaining your hydroponic gardening system is important to protecting your plant's health (guarding against disease) and to clear the system of precipitates such as calcium and other minerals that may be in your water/nutrient solution.

How often you clean your entire system is entirely up to you. Some hydroponic gardeners will maintain that you should cleanse your system after each harvest. This is a costly and time-consuming proposition.

It is not necessary that you clean your system after each crop is harvested. A good rule is to maintain records of how much water/nutrient solution you use to top off your system each time you have to add it to keep the levels up. Once you reach the point that you have added half the amount that the reservoir holds (example: If your bucket holds four gallons, your replacement amount would peak at two gallons of water/nutrient solution), you then would allow the water/nutrient solution to dissipate naturally to the point where you would need to top it off again and then prepare an entire new batch. At this point, you can clean the entire system.

It is vital that you keep a sharp eye on your system and the plants to determine if there is a problem related to cleanliness, bacteria, or algae. If so, it will be necessary to clean the system rather than wait until you have reached that two-gallon limit.

After you have determined it is time to clean your system, dismantle the system by removing the plants, the plant mesh pots, and the Leca from the bucket lid.

Remove the reservoir lid from the reservoir and discard the water/nutrient solution.

Clean all components with hot water and a good sanitizer such as Star San.

Fill the reservoir and the plant buckets with water and add household bleach at a level of four teaspoons per gallon of water.

Mix the bleach into the water and allow to soak for 24 to 72 hours.

While the system is soaking, run the pump in 15-minute cycles every hour to clean the hoses.

After the reservoir and plant buckets have soaked, discard the bleach solution, and flush the whole system several times with fresh water to rid the system of the bleach and any other materials dislodged by the cleaning.

If you choose to use tap water to flush your system, be sure that you allow the water to sit for 24 hours before using the water to allow any chlorine in the water to dissipate.

If you notice a build-up of precipitates such as calcium on the sides of your reservoir or in your pump unit, you may need to do an acid flush of the system.

For an acid flush:

Add water and hydrochloric acid at the rate of ¾ teaspoon per gallon of water to the reservoir. Your goal is to achieve a pH of 2.

Allow the reservoir to soak for 24 to 72 hours.

While the system is soaking, run the pump at least 15 minutes in every hour.

After the system has finished soaking, neutralize the soak water flushing solution to pH 5 to 6 with soda ash before discarding it.

Flush the whole system several times with fresh water to rid the system of the acid solution and any other materials dislodged by the cleaning.

If you choose to use tap water to flush your system, be sure that you allow the water to sit for 24 hours before using the water to allow any chlorine in the water to dissipate.

If you choose to use tap water as the basis for your water/nutrient solution, draw the water, and allow it to sit for 24 hours. This allows the chlorine to dissipate.

Allow the water/nutrient solution to rest for two hours after you mix the nutrients into the water before you check the pH level. You get a more accurate pH reading this way

Keep a thermometer near your hydroponic gardening system to help maintain the temperature between 60 and 80 degrees. Adhesive thermometer strips that you apply directly to your reservoir are available. Alternatively, you can use an aquarium thermometer, but as it will be inside the reservoir, it will be difficult to read. If the water/nutrient solution gets too warm, you risk breeding bacteria that is bad for the plant's roots.

Put a small amount (a few drops) of hydrogen peroxide into your reservoir on a weekly basis. This will deter the growth of bacteria and algae.

Always check to make sure that the pump is running. If the pump stops, the water will become stagnant, and bacteria will start to grow. Also, the plant roots need the oxygen provided by the pump.

Always be sure that your pump is above the level of the reservoir so if your power goes out, there is no negative backflow into the pump.

Enclose the end of your pump hose in a screen to keep debris out of it.

Maintaining system cleanliness is vital to the health and wellbeing of your plants and your system. Keep a record of your cleaning. This will allow for greatest system efficiency.

The resource directory in the back of this book will direct you to supplies to help you maintain the cleanliness of your system and the health of your plants. Chapter 10 will go into greater detail about ongoing maintenance issues of your hydroponic gardening system and your plants.

As mentioned earlier, dynamic hydroponic gardening systems are systems that recirculate the liquid nutrient solution through the system as long as the system is viable.

Ebb-and-Flow Hydroponic System

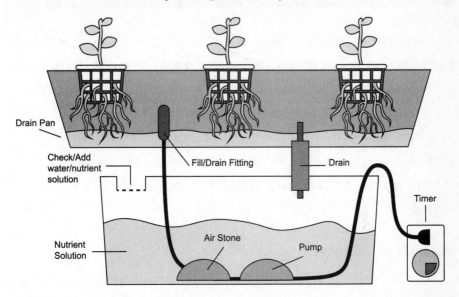

The ebb-and-flow hydroponic gardening system, also called the flood-and-drain system, is aptly named because it does just what the name suggests. The system uses a pump connected to a timer. The timer allows the pump to send water on a regular schedule from the reservoir that holds the water/nutrient solution to a pan, called a drain pan, which contains the pots that hold the plants. The drain pan is fitted with an overflow drain, allowing the drain pan to be flooded to a level that will water and feed the plants. As the pump sends the water/nutrient solution to the drain pan, it also drains the overflow back into the reservoir that contains the water/nutrient solution. As such, the ebb-and-flow hydroponic gardening system is considered a dynamic system.

The basic design of the ebb-and-flow hydroponic gardening system is very similar to the wick system described earlier in this chapter in that the basic system components are much the same. The system described here will be constructed using two storage totes, though these totes will be slightly different in size, with the reservoir being somewhat deeper than the drain pan.

This system creates a tidal effect, periodically flooding the root chambers with nutrient solution and then letting it drain back away. These are the most common systems for larger gardens once you have gone past the initial beginner stage. After the trays in which the plants are situated are flooded, the nutrient solution is allowed to drain. The drained nutrient solution in this dynamic system is collected and recirculated as long as the nutrient solution is viable.

Materials you will need:

- Reservoir pan (To keep this system as simple as possible, you can use just about any reservoir that has a lid or can accommodate a lid and is big enough to accommodate the plants you want to grow. The ideal reservoir might be a plastic storage tote with a lid, though this reservoir could be as simple as a large mayonnaise jar, a plastic bucket, or a cooler. These instructions will employ a plastic storage tote that is 18" x 23" x 21" [W x L x D] or approximately 17 gallons. You will need to be able to place the drain pan on top of the reservoir. Like the raft system reservoir, you will want to make any reservoir you employ in this system opaque to make sure sunlight cannot penetrate into the water/nutrient solution.)
- Reservoir lid (This needs to be a tight-fitting lid that fits snuggly in place on top if the reservoir you have chosen. Ideally, you have chosen a reservoir that has its own custom lid.)

- Drain pan (Ideally, the drain pan should be smaller in length and width to the reservoir pan, and it should be shallower — 11" x 16" x 7" [W x H x D] or approximately four gallons. The drain pan will sit on top of the reservoir. If the two containers are of a similar construction and manufactured as stackable units, the construction of this ebb-and-flow system is made easier.)
- Plant pan lid (Like the reservoir lid, this needs to be a tight-fitting lid that fits snuggly in place on top if the plant pan you have chosen. Ideally, you have chosen a plant pan that has its own custom lid. Alternatively, the system may be constructed without a lid for the drain pan.)
- Timer, mechanical garden (Ideally, you will want a timer that you can set in 15-minute increments.)
- Aquarium air pump
- Six feet of airline tubing
- "T" connector
- Airstone
- Four to six 2" mesh cups
- Growing medium (You may use the lightweight expanded clay aggregate [Leca] you may have used in the raft system, or you can choose to go with a medium that has wicking ability, such as rock wool or perlite. A combination of materials such as vermiculite, perlite, and coconut coir would also be a good choice. This material is used as an anchor for the plant roots).
- Black irrigation tubing (tubing with a ½" inner diameter and about 18 inches long)
- Small submersible pump (The pump needed here is one you might find in a garden pond. An example of such a

pump is Little Giant PE-A that pumps at 80 gallons/
hour or a PES-A that pumps at 63 gallons/hour.
Pumps such as these sell for $45 to $60 at garden shops
or online retailers.)

- Fill-and-drain fitting set with one extension (These two
  plumbing pieces allow the water/nutrient solution to be
  pumped into the drain pan and then to drain out. One of
  the pieces is a short pipe that is attached to the pump in
  the reservoir tank. The second piece is taller and acts as
  an overflow drainpipe.)
- 1" x 1" stick or a wood dowel about three feet long

Tools you will need:

- Electric or battery-powered drill
- ³/₈" or ½" chuck 1¼" hole saws for cutting plant sites
- Jigsaw or coping saw for cutting holes in the reservoir lid
- Razor knife for cutting tubing and rope
- Sandpaper
- A pen or marker

Instructions:

- Use the 1¼" hole saw of the drill to cut two 1¼-inch holes
  near the center of the drain pan. Sand the rough edges of
  the holes you cut to smooth them out.
- Put the drain pan on top of lid of the reservoir (If the
  units were not made to stack, make sure that the drain
  pan is centered on the reservoir lid). Use a pen or a
  marker to mark to trace the two cut holes of the drain
  pan on the lid of the reservoir.
- Use the 1¼" hole saw of the drill to cut two 1¼" holes in
  the lid of the reservoir where marked. (The holes of the

drain pan should be lined up exactly with the holes of the reservoir lid.)

- Use the 1¼" hole saw of the drill to cut two more 1¼" holes in the lid of the reservoir, one on each of the short sides lid. (One of the holes will be for the pump power cord and tubing to pass through. The other hole will be to check and add to the water/nutrient solution after the system is put together.)
- Screw, by hand, the fill-and-drain fitting set, with the one extension added to the drainpipe, into the holes of the bottom of the drain pan. The fittings will come with gaskets that will go on the underside of the drain pan. Tighten these gaskets by hand.
- Fit the ½" irrigation tubing on the water pump outlet opening. The fit should be tight. If the fit seems loose, you can use couplers with screws or zip ties to tighten the tubing to the pump outlet opening.
- Fit the drain pan, with the fittings in place, over the lid of the reservoir (the lid should be off the reservoir at this point), make sure that the holes are lined up, and that the fittings go through the lid.
- Set the water pump on the bottom of the reservoir to measure and trim the ½" black tubing to attach to the fill pipe that has been screwed into the drain pan and reservoir lid when the lid is on the reservoir.
- Place the tubing over the port of the fill pipe (the shorter drainpipe) from the bottom of the reservoir lid. The fit should be tight. If the fit seems loose, you can use couplers with screws or zip ties to tighten the tubing.)
- The water pump will be plugged into the timer that, in turn, will be plugged into a power outlet. The timer will

be set according to the levels of moisture that your plants demand.

- Place the airstone into the bottom of the reservoir, and run the airline tubing and the power cord to the aquarium pump plug through the side holes you drilled into the sides of the reservoir lid.
- Fit the lid/drain pan assembly on top of the reservoir, and snap into place.
- Make a "dipstick" out of the 1" x 1" stick or a wood dowel to be used to measure the water/nutrient solution in the reservoir. As you first add water/nutrient solution to the reservoir through one of the holes you drilled in the side of the reservoir lid, do so one gallon at a time. After each gallon, put the stick into the reservoir. Use a marker to mark the gallon level on the stick. You then will have an accurate way to measure water/nutrient levels without having to remove the drain pan and lid assembly each time you measure levels.
- Fill the reservoir with 12 gallons of water/nutrient solution.
- Turn on the aquarium pump and water pump to test the system for any leaks.
- If the system is leak free, you are ready to plant.
- If the system has any leaks, they probably will be where the aquarium pump joins the hose, address them by tightening hoses.
- The growing medium in this system will be placed in the mesh cups inside the drain pan when you are ready to plant.

Maintaining your hydroponic ebb-and-flow system:

Maintaining your hydroponic gardening system is important to protecting your plant's health (guarding against disease) and to clear the system of precipitates such as calcium and other minerals that may be in your water/nutrient solution.

How often you clean your entire system is entirely up to you. Some hydroponic gardeners maintain that you should cleanse your system after each harvest. This is a costly and time-consuming proposition.

It is not necessary that you clean your system after each crop is harvested. A good rule is to maintain records of how much water/nutrient solution you use to top off your system each time you have to add it to keep the levels up. Once you reach the point that you have added half the amount that the reservoir holds (example: if your reservoir holds 34 gallons, your replacement amount would peak at 17 gallons of water/nutrient solution), you then would allow the water/nutrient solution to dissipate naturally to the point where you would need to top it off again and then prepare an entire new batch. At this point, you can clean the entire system.

It is vital that you keep a sharp eye on your system and the plants to determine if there is a problem related to cleanliness, bacteria, or algae. If so, it will be necessary to clean the system rather than wait until you have reached that 17-gallon limit.

After you have determined it is time to clean your system, dismantle the system by removing the plants, the mesh pots, and the growing medium.

Discard the water/nutrient solution.

Clean all components with hot water and a good sanitizer such as Star San.

Fill the reservoir and the drain pan with water and add household bleach at a level of four (4) teaspoons per gallon of water.

Mix the bleach into the water, and allow to soak for 24 to 72 hours.

While the system is soaking, run the pump in 15-minute cycles every hour to clean the hoses.

After the reservoir and drain pan have soaked, discard the bleach solution and flush the whole system several times with fresh water to rid the system of the bleach and any other materials dislodged by the cleaning.

If you choose to use tap water to flush your system, be sure that you have allowed the water to sit for 24 hours before using the water to allow any chlorine in the water to dissipate.

If you notice a build-up of precipitates such as calcium on the sides of your reservoir or in your pump unit, you may need to do an acid flush if the system.

For an acid flush:

Add water and hydrochloric acid at the rate of ¾ teaspoon per gallon of water to the reservoir and drain pan. Your goal is to achieve a pH of 2.

Allow the reservoir and drain pan to soak for 24 to 72 hours.

While the system is soaking, run the pump at least 15 minutes in every hour.

After the system is done soaking, neutralize the soak water flushing solution to pH 5 to 6 with soda ash before discarding it.

Flush the whole system several times with fresh water to rid the system of the acid solution and any other materials dislodged by the cleaning.

If you choose to use tap water to flush your system, be sure that you have allowed the water to sit for 24 hours before using the water to allow any chlorine in the water to dissipate.

If you choose to use tap water as the basis for your water/nutrient solution, draw the water and allow it to sit for 24 hours. This allows the chlorine to dissipate.

Allow the water/nutrient solution to rest for two hours after you mix the nutrients into the water before you check the pH level. You get a more accurate pH reading this way

Keep a thermometer near your hydroponic gardening system to help maintain the temperature between 60 and 80 degrees. Adhesive thermometer strips that you apply directly to your reservoir are available. Alternatively, you can use an aquarium thermometer, but as it will be inside the reservoir, it will be difficult to read. If the water/nutrient solution gets too warm, you risk breeding bacteria that is bad for the plant's roots.

Put a small amount (a few drops) of hydrogen peroxide into your reservoir on a weekly basis. This will deter the growth of bacteria and algae.

Always check to make sure that the pump is running. If the pump stops, the water will become stagnant, and bacteria will start to grow. Also, the plant roots need the oxygen provided by the pump.

Always be sure that your pump is above the level of the reservoir so that if your power goes out, there is no negative backflow into the pump. Enclose the end of your pump hose in a screen to keep debris out of it.

Maintaining system cleanliness is vital to the health and well-being of your plants and your system. Keep a record of your cleaning. This will allow for greatest system efficiency.

The resource directory in the back of this book will direct you to supplies to help you maintain the cleanliness of your system and the health of your plants. Chapter 10 will go into greater detail related to ongoing maintenance issues of your hydroponic gardening system and your plants.

Nutrient-Film-Technique System

The nutrient-film-technique (NFT) hydroponic gardening system is, perhaps, the most efficient and effective system described yet. NFT, though, is a more advanced system than the others that have been described. Because of that, if you are new to hydroponic gardening, you should experiment with other systems before attempting to construct and employ this advanced NFT hydroponic gardening system.

As its name implies, NFT works by providing a thin film of water/nutrient solution to the plants. This is done in a dynamic manner as the water/nutrient film moves through the system, is collected in a reservoir, and is then recirculated through the system anew.

There are many different designs for NFT systems. NFT systems are the types of systems most frequently used by commercial hydroponic growers, as long channels of PVC piping can contain hundreds and hundreds of plants being fed by the same reservoir of water/nutrient solution.

The basic idea of the NFT hydroponic gardening system is that a pump connected to a reservoir containing a water/nutrient solution pumps the nutrient to a tray or channel containing the plants. The tray/channel is built on a bit of an incline to allow the water/nutrient solution to run downhill and through the roots of the plants. At the end of the tray/channel is a drain that allows the water/nutrient solution to drain back into the reservoir to be recirculated through the system.

The NFT system described here is similar in construction to the ebb-and-flow system described before with a couple important alterations to the drain pan and the movement of the water/nutrient solution. As the water/nutrient solution needs to flow through the drain pan evenly and at a regular rate, the drain pan needs to be constructed to allow the water/nutrient solution to do so. Also, the drain pan for this system should be somewhat shallower than the drain pan for the ebb-and-flow systems.

Materials you will need:

- Reservoir pan (To keep this system as simple as possible, you can use just about any reservoir that has a lid or can accommodate a lid and is big enough to accommodate the plants you want to grow. The ideal reservoir might be a plastic storage tote with a lid, though this reservoir could be as simple as a large mayonnaise jar, a plastic bucket, or a cooler. These instructions will employ a plastic storage tote that is 18" x 23" x 21" [W x L x D] or approximately 17 gallons. You will need to be able to place the drain pan on top of the reservoir. Like the raft system reservoir, you will want to make any reservoir you employ in this system opaque to make sure sunlight cannot penetrate into the water/nutrient solution.)
- Reservoir lid (This needs to be a tight-fitting lid that fits snuggly in place on top if the reservoir you have chosen.

Ideally, you have chosen a reservoir that has its own custom lid.)

- Drain pan (Ideally, the drain pan should be a shallow plastic tote that is roughly the same width and length of the reservoir, but is very shallow. Sterlite® sells a 28-quart tote ideal for this construction and is available through Home Depot® or at many online retailers. This tote is 16¼" x 23" x 6" [W x L x D]. The drain pan will sit on top of the reservoir. If the two containers are of a similar construction and manufactured as stackable units, the construction of this NFT system is made easier.)
- Plant pan lid (Like the reservoir lid, this needs to be a tight-fitting lid that fits snuggly in place on top if the plant pan you have chosen. Ideally, you have chosen a plant pan that has its own custom lid. Alternatively, the system may be constructed without a lid for the drain pan.)
- PVC pipe (This pipe will 2" diameter and will be cut to fit the width and sit on the floor of the drain pan.)
- Silicone caulk
- Timer, mechanical garden (Ideally, you will want a timer that you can set in 15-minute increments.)
- Aquarium air pump
- Six feet of airline tubing
- "T" connector
- Airstone
- Four to six 2" mesh cups
- Growing medium (You may use the lightweight expanded clay aggregate [Leca] you may have used in the raft system or you can choose to go with a medium that has wicking ability, such as rock wool or perlite. A combination of materials such as vermiculite, perlite, and

coconut coir would also be a good choice. This material is used as an anchor for the plant roots).

- Black irrigation tubing (tubing with a ½" inner diameter and about 18 inches long)
- Small submersible pump (The pump needed here is one you might find in a garden pond. An example of such a pump is Little Giant PE-A that pumps at 80 gallons/hour or a PES-A that pumps at 63 gallons/hour. Pumps such as these sell for $45 to $60 at garden shops or online retailers.)
- Fill-and-drain fitting set with one extension (These two plumbing pieces allow the water/nutrient solution to be pumped into the drain pan and then to drain out. One of the pieces is a short pipe attached to the pump in the reservoir tank. The second piece acts as a drainpipe. The extension may be necessary to add to the fill pipe if the incline of the drain pan demands it. Remember. The side of the drain pan where the water/nutrient solution enters is raised slightly to allow the flow of solution through the drain pan.)
- Shims (These are small angled pieces of wood that will sit under the drain pan to give it a slight incline. Shims are readily available in hardware stores in packages of 20, or so. You will have to experiment with the precise number you will need, but one package should be plenty as you will not need any more than six to eight.)
- 1" x 1" stick or a wood dowel about three inches long

Tools you will need:

- Electric or battery-powered drill
- ³/₈" or ½" chuck 1¼" hole saws for cutting plant sites

- Jigsaw or coping saw for cutting holes in the drain pan lid
- Razor knife for cutting tubing and rope
- Sandpaper
- A pen or marker

Instructions:

- Use the 1¼" hole saw of the drill to cut two 1¼" holes. One hole at the center of each end of the drain pan. Sand the rough edges of the holes you cut to smooth them out.
- Put the drain pan on top of lid of the reservoir (if the units were not made to stack, make sure that the drain pan is centered on the reservoir lid). Use a pen or a marker to mark to trace the two cut holes of the drain pan on the lid of the reservoir.
- Use the 1¼" hole saw of the drill to cut two 1¼" holes in the lid of the reservoir where marked. (The holes of the drain pan should be lined up exactly with the holes of the reservoir lid.)
- Use the 1¼" hole saw of the drill to cut one more 1¼" hole in the side of the lid of the reservoir. This hole should be cut in the center of one of the length sides. (The hole will be for the pump power cord and tubing to pass through.)
- Screw, by hand, the fill-and-drain fitting set, with the one extension added to the drainpipe, into the holes of the bottom of the drain pan. The fittings will come with gaskets that will go on the underside of the drain pan. Tighten these gaskets by hand. The fill fitting will go into one end of the drain pan, and the drain fitting will go into the other side of the drain pan.

- Measure and cut the PVC pipe so it fits the width of the drain pan and sits snuggly into the bottom of the drain pan about two inches from the fill fitting (closer to the center of the drain pan than the fill fitting).

- Place the PVC two inches from the fill fitting and caulk with the silicone caulk along the bottom length and at the sides of the PVC (The PVC and silicone caulk will act as a dam to ensure that the flow of water/nutrient solution is evenly distributed along the width of the drain pan.)

- Fit the ½" irrigation tubing on the water pump outlet opening. The fit should be tight. If the fit seems loose, you can use couplers with screws or zip ties to tighten the tubing to the pump outlet opening.

- Fit the drain pan, with the fittings in place, over the lid of the reservoir. As you take this step, put four shims (two on each side) of the fill side of the drain pan between the drain pan and the reservoir lid (the lid should be off of the reservoir at this point). You want to be sure that the fill side of the drain pan is slightly elevated. You may need to adjust the elevation once you get the system up and running to speed up or slow down the flow of water/nutrient solution. Make sure that the holes are lined up and that the fittings go through the lid.

- Set the water pump on the bottom of the reservoir to measure and trim the ½" black tubing to attach to the fill pipe that has been screwed into the drain pan and reservoir lid when the lid is on the reservoir.

- Place the tubing over the port of the fill pipe from the bottom of the reservoir lid. (The fit should be tight. If the fit seems loose, you can use couplers with screws or zip ties to tighten the tubing.)

- The water pump will be plugged into the timer that, in turn, will be plugged into a power outlet. The timer will be set according to the levels of moisture that your plants demand.
- Place the airstone into the bottom of the reservoir, and run the airline tubing and the power cord to the aquarium pump plug through the side holes you drilled into the sides of the reservoir lid.
- Fit the lid/drain pan assembly on top of the reservoir, and snap into place.
- Trace the bottoms of the mesh cups on the lid of the drain pan. Whether you use four or six mesh cups, make sure that the cups will be evenly spaced in the lid of the pan.
- Cut the four to six holes in the drain pan lid with the jigsaw. The mesh cups should be able to sit on or just barely off of the bottom of the drain pan, no more than 1/16" off the bottom.
- Fill the reservoir with 12 gallons of water/nutrient solution.
- Turn on the aquarium pump and water pump to test the system for any leaks and the flow of the water/nutrient solution through the drain pan.
- If the system is leak free, place the drain pan lid on the drain pan.
- If the system has any leaks, they probably will be where the aquarium pump joins the hose, address them by tightening hoses. Address these leaks by tightening hoses.
- The growing medium in this system will be placed in mesh cups inside the drain pan lid when you are ready to plant.

Maintaining your NFT system:

Maintaining your hydroponic gardening system is important to protecting your plant's health (guarding against disease) and to clear the system of precipitates such as calcium and other minerals that may be in your water/nutrient solution.

How often you clean your entire system is entirely up to you. Some will maintain that you should cleanse your system after each harvest. This is a costly and time-consuming proposition.

It is not necessary for you clean your system after each crop is harvested. A good rule is to maintain records of how much water/nutrient solution you use to top off your system each time you have to add it to keep the levels up. Once you reach the point that you have added half the amount that the reservoir holds (example: if your reservoir holds 34 gallons, your replacement amount would peak at 17 gallons of water/nutrient solution), you then would allow the water/nutrient solution to dissipate naturally to the point where you would need to top it off again and then prepare an entire new batch. At this point, you can clean the entire system.

It is vital that you keep a sharp eye on your system and the plants to determine if there is a problem related to cleanliness, bacteria, or algae. If so, it will be necessary to clean the system rather than wait until you have reached that 17-gallon limit.

After you have determined it is time to clean your system, dismantle the system by removing the plants, the mesh pots, and the growing medium.

Discard the water/nutrient solution.

Clean all components with hot water and a good sanitizer such as Star San.

Fill the reservoir and the drain pan with water and add household bleach at a level of four teaspoons per gallon of water.

Mix the bleach into the water and allow to soak for 24 to 72 hours.

While the system is soaking, run the pump in 15-minute cycles every hour to clean the hoses.

After the reservoir and drain pan have soaked, discard the bleach solution, and flush the whole system several times with fresh water to rid the system of bleach and any other materials dislodged by the cleaning.

If you choose to use tap water to flush your system, be sure you have allowed the water to sit for 24 hours before using the water to allow any chlorine in the water to dissipate.

If you notice that there is a build-up of precipitates such as calcium on the sides of your reservoir or in your pump unit, you may need to do an acid flush if the system.

For an acid flush:

Add water and hydrochloric acid at the rate of ¾ teaspoon per gallon of water to the reservoir and drain pan. Your goal is to achieve a pH of 2.

Allow the reservoir and drain pan to soak for 24 to 72 hours.

While the system is soaking, run the pump at least 15 minutes in every hour.

After the system has finished soaking, neutralize the soak water flushing solution to pH 5 to 6 with soda ash before discarding it.

Flush the whole system several times with fresh water to rid the system of the acid solution and any other materials dislodged by the cleaning.

If you choose to use tap water to flush your system, be sure that you have allowed the water to sit for 24 hours before using the water to allow any chlorine in the water to dissipate.

If you choose to use tap water as the basis for your water/nutrient solution, draw the water and allow it to sit for 24 hours. This allows the chlorine to dissipate.

Allow the water/nutrient solution to rest for two hours after you mix the nutrients into the water before you check the pH level. You get a more accurate pH reading this way

Keep a thermometer near your hydroponic gardening system to help maintain the temperature between 60 and 80 degrees. Adhesive thermometer strips that you apply directly to your reservoir are available. Alternatively, you can use an aquarium thermometer, but as it will be inside the reservoir, it will be difficult to read. If the water/nutrient solution gets too warm, you risk breeding bacteria that is bad for the plant's roots.

Put a small amount (a few drops) of hydrogen peroxide into your reservoir on a weekly basis. This will deter the growth of bacteria and algae.

Always check to make sure that the pump is running. If the pump stops, the water will become stagnant, and bacteria will start to grow. Also, the plant roots need the oxygen provided by the pump.

Always be sure that your pump is above the level of the reservoir so if your power goes out, there is no negative backflow into the pump. Enclose the end of your pump hose in a screen to keep debris out of it.

Maintaining system cleanliness is vital to the health and well-being of your plants and your system. Keep a record of your cleaning. This will allow for greatest system efficiency.

The resource directory in the back of this book will direct you to supplies to help you maintain the cleanliness of your system and the health of your plants. Chapter 10 will go into greater detail about ongoing maintenance issues of your hydroponic gardening system and your plants.

Aeroponics

An aeroponic approach is significantly different than the others because you are not working with liquid nutrient solutions in the same way. Your plants are suspended in their mesh pots, but their roots hang loose in a large open chamber. Frequently through the day, solution is misted or sprayed into the chamber to nourish and moisten the roots. In this way, you achieve the same goal of using a soil-less method of delivering nutrients to your plants.

Aeroponic systems are included here as a dynamic system because the more sophisticated aeroponic systems will recirculate the nutrient-rich mist that feeds the plants with a system of pumps and fans.

Materials you will need:

- Reservoir pan (These instructions will employ a plastic storage tote 18″ x 23″ x 21″ [W x L x D] or approximately 17 gallons. You will need to be able to place the drain pan on top of the reservoir. Like the raft-system reservoir, you will want to make any reservoir you employ in this system opaque to make sure sunlight cannot penetrate into the water/nutrient solution.)
- Reservoir lid (This needs to be a tight-fitting lid that fits snuggly in place on top if the reservoir you have chosen. Ideally, you have chosen a reservoir that has its own custom lid.)
- Drain pan (Ideally, the drain pan should be the same plastic storage tote 18″ x 23″ x 21″ [W x L x D] or approximately 17 gallons that the reservoir is. The drain

pan will sit on top of the reservoir. If the two containers
are of a similar construction and manufactured as
stackable units, the construction of this aeroponic system
is made easier.)

- Plant pan lid (Like the reservoir lid, this needs to be a
  tight-fitting lid that fits snuggly in place on top if the plant
  pan you have chosen. Ideally, you have chosen a plant
  pan that has its own custom lid. Alternatively, the system
  may be constructed without a lid for the drain pan.)
- Garden mister (This is a short flexible misting hose
  generally used to provide heat relief to people. A good
  option is the Orbit FlexCobra Mistand Mister. Any small
  garden mister that attaches to a garden hose and fits into
  the bottom of the drain pan will work.)
- Short length of ⁵/₈"-diameter garden hose with fittings
  on both ends (You can cut longer hose lengths down to
  accommodate your needs and attach fittings yourself
  with kits you can get from your local hardware store,
  or you might be able to have the hardware store put
  fittings on for you, The hose only needs to be about three
  inches long to run from the pump in the reservoir to the
  mister in the drain pan. If you do not want to mess with
  cutting hose and putting on fittings, you can purchase a
  ⁵/₈"-diameter, 6' hose reel leader hose that will work fine.)
- Timer, mechanical garden; (Ideally, you will want a timer
  that you can set in 15-minute increments.)
- Aquarium air pump
- Six feet of airline tubing
- "T" connector
- Airstone
- Four to six 2" mesh cups

- Small submersible pump (The pump needed here is one you might find in a garden pond. An example of such a pump is Little Giant PE-A that pumps at 80 gallons/hour or a PES-A that pumps at 63 gallons/hour. Pumps such as these sell for $45 to $60 at garden shops or online retailers.)
- Drain-fitting set (This plumbing piece will allow the water/nutrient solution to be drained out of the drain pan.)
- Plumber's putty
- Shims (These are small angled pieces of wood that will sit under the drain pan to give it a slight incline. Shims are readily available in hardware stores in packages of 20, or so. You will have to experiment with the precise number you will need, but one package should be plenty as you will not need any more than six to eight.)
- 1" x 1" stick or a wood dowel about three feet long

Tools you will need:
- Electric or battery-powered drill
- ³/₈" or ½" chuck 1¼" hole saws for cutting plant sites
- Jigsaw or coping saw for cutting holes in the reservoir lid
- Razor knife for cutting tubing and rope
- Sandpaper
- A pen or marker

Instructions:
- Use the 1¼" hole saw of the drill to cut two 1¼" holes. One hole at the center of the drain pan and one hole at the center of one of the ends of the drain pan. Sand the rough edges of the holes you cut to smooth them out.

- Put the drain pan on top of lid of the reservoir (if the units were not made to stack, make sure that the drain pan is centered on the reservoir lid). Use a pen or a marker to mark to trace the two cut holes of the drain pan on the lid of the reservoir.
- Use the 1¼" hole saw of the drill to cut two 1¼" holes in the lid of the reservoir where marked. (The holes of the drain pan should be lined up exactly with the holes of the reservoir lid.)
- Use the 1¼" hole saw of the drill to cut one more 1¼" hole in the side of the lid of the reservoir. This hole should be cut in the center of one of the length sides. (The hole will be for the pump power cord and tubing to pass through.)
- Screw, by hand, the drain-fitting set, with the one extension added to the drainpipe, into the. The fitting will come with a gasket that will go on the underside of the drain pan. Tighten the gasket by hand.
- Fit the garden hose fitting on the water pump outlet opening. The fit should be tight.
- Fit the drain pan, with the drain fitting in place over the lid of the reservoir (The lid should be off of the reservoir at this point), and make sure that the holes are lined up and that the fittings go through the lid.
- Set the water pump on the bottom of the reservoir to measure and trim the garden hose if necessary to run from the reservoir up into the drain pan. Excess hose can be coiled in the drain pan.
- Run the garden hose through the center hole of the reservoir lid and the center hole of the drain pan.

- Place the mister in the center of the drain pan and attach the garden hose to the mister.
- Fill the space around the bottom of the drain pan where the garden hose comes into the drain pan with plumber's putty to halt any leakage possibility.
- The water pump will be plugged into the timer that, in turn, will be plugged into a power outlet. The timer will be set according to the levels of moisture that you plants demand.
- Place the airstone into the bottom of the reservoir, and run the airline tubing and the power cord to the aquarium pump plug through the side holes you drilled into the sides of the reservoir lid.
- Fit the lid/drain pan assembly on top of the reservoir, and snap into place.
- Cut the four to six holes in the drain pan lid with the jigsaw. The mesh cups should be suspended about three to four inches inside the drain pan
- Fill the reservoir with 12 gallons of water/nutrient solution.
- Turn on the aquarium pump and water pump to test the system for any leaks.
- If the system is leak free, you are ready to plant.
- If the system has any leaks, they will probably be where the aquarium pump joins the hoses. Address these leaks by tightening hoses.
- The growing medium in this system will be placed in mesh cups inside the drain pan when you are ready to plant.

Maintaining your aeroponic system:

Maintaining your hydroponic gardening system is important to protecting your plant's health (guarding against disease) and to clear the system of precipitates such as calcium and other minerals that may be in your water/nutrient solution.

How often you clean your entire system is entirely up to you. Some hydroponic gardeners maintain that you should cleanse your system after each harvest. This is a costly and time-consuming proposition.

It is not necessary for you clean your system after each crop is harvested. A good rule is to maintain records of how much water/nutrient solution you use to top off your system each time you have to add it to keep the levels up. Once you reach the point that you have added half the amount that the reservoir holds (example: if your reservoir holds 34 gallons, your replacement amount would peak at 17 gallons of water/nutrient solution), you then would allow the water/nutrient solution to dissipate naturally to the point where you would need to top it off again and then prepare an entire new batch. At this point, you can clean the entire system.

It is vital that you keep a sharp eye on your system and the plants to determine if there is a problem related to cleanliness, bacteria, or algae. If so, it will be necessary to clean the system rather than wait until you have reached that 17-gallon limit.

After you have determined it is time to clean your system, dismantle the system by removing the plants, the mesh pots, and the growing medium.

Discard the water/nutrient solution.

Clean all components with hot water and a good sanitizer such as Star San.

Fill the reservoir and the drain pan with water, and add household bleach at a level of four teaspoons per gallon of water.

Mix the bleach into the water and soak for 24 to 72 hours.

While the system is soaking, run the pump in 15-minute cycles every hour to clean the hoses.

After the reservoir and drain pan have soaked, discard the bleach solution and flush the whole system several times with fresh water to rid the system of the bleach and any other materials dislodged by the cleaning.

If you choose to use tap water to flush your system, be sure that you have allowed the water to sit for 24 hours before to using the water to allow any chlorine in the water to dissipate.

If you notice a build-up of precipitates such as calcium on the sides of your reservoir or in your pump unit, you may need to do an acid flush if the system.

For an acid flush:

Add water and hydrochloric acid at the rate of ¾ teaspoon per gallon of water to the reservoir and drain pan. Your goal is to achieve a pH of 2. Allow the reservoir and drain pan to soak for 24 to 72 hours.

While the system is soaking, run the pump at least 15 minutes in every hour.

After the system is done soaking, neutralize the soak water flushing solution to pH 5 to 6 with soda ash before discarding it.

Flush the whole system several times with fresh water to rid the system of the acid solution and any other materials dislodged by the cleaning.

If you choose to use tap water to flush your system, be sure that you have allowed the water to sit for 24 hours before using the water to allow any chlorine in the water to dissipate.

If you choose to use tap water as the basis for your water/nutrient solution, draw the water and allow it to sit for 24 hours. This allows the chlorine to dissipate.

Allow the water/nutrient solution to rest for two hours after you mix the nutrients into the water before you check the pH level. You get a more accurate pH reading this way

Keep a thermometer near your hydroponic gardening system to help maintain the temperature between 60 and 80 degrees. Adhesive thermometer strips that you apply directly to your reservoir are available. Alternatively, you can use an aquarium thermometer, but as it will be inside the reservoir, it will be difficult to read. If the water/nutrient solution gets too warm, you risk breeding bacteria that is bad for the plant's roots. Put a small amount (a few drops) of hydrogen peroxide into your reservoir on a weekly basis. This will deter the growth of bacteria and algae.

Always check to make sure that the pump is running. If the pump stops, the water will become stagnant, and bacteria will start to grow. Also, the plant roots need the oxygen provided by the pump.

Always be sure that your pump is above the level of the reservoir so if your power goes out, there is no negative backflow into the pump. Enclose the end of your pump hose in a screen to keep debris out of it.

Maintaining system cleanliness is vital to the health and well-being of your plants and your system. Keep a record of your cleaning. This will allow for greatest system efficiency.

The resource directory in the back of this book will direct you to supplies to help you maintain the cleanliness of your system and the health of your plants. Chapter 10 will go into greater detail about ongoing maintenance issues of your hydroponic gardening system and your plants.

Do-It-Yourself or Ready Made?

All of the descriptions outlined in this chapter have detailed hydroponic gardening systems that you can build yourself. The systems described range from the ultra-simple sprouts grown in a jar to the more complex aeroponic misting systems. You may have noted, if you read through the descriptions of all of the individual systems, that many of them have similar designs and employ much of the same equipment. One of the biggest upsides to building a system yourself is that you may acquire equipment necessary to construct not one hydroponic gardening system but two or even three different types of systems. You also will gain a greater understanding of how, exactly, a specific system works.

If, on the other hand, you want to launch immediately into hydroponic gardening and you do not want to experiment with constructing your own system, any one of the systems described in this chapter is available from any number of online retailers that deal in hydroponic gardening systems. Most of the systems will come with just about everything you will require to get your hydroponic gardening up and running right out of the box. Some systems even may come with plants ready to be put into the system.

The resource section in the back of this book will direct you online retailers that deal in ready-made hydroponic gardening systems, as well as components to help you build your own system.

CASE STUDY: MARV FRITZ

Marv Fritz, Operations Manager
Garden Fresh Vegetables
P.O. Box 300
O'Neill, NE 68763
Office 402-336-4800

Marv Fritz is the operations manager at Garden Fresh Vegetables in O'Neill, Nebraska. Fritz became interested in hydroponics because he saw it as the future of agriculture. He saw that with hydroponics, we can feed more people on less acreage and use less water. Garden Fresh Vegetables grows fresh tomatoes and cucumbers year-round. The greenhouse process is designed to ripen produce naturally, not through artificial chemicals.

Garden Fresh Vegetables is a 24-acre, glass Venlo-type greenhouse. The Venlo-type greenhouse is a popular design for greenhouses among professional growers. The design's primary feature is a truss-mounted ventilation system operated via a push-pull rail mechanic, with roof vents on both sides of the ridge-topped roof. The roof vents are operated separately. This greenhouse design is highly economical, as it is suitable for all crops in most climate conditions. The Venlo style of greenhouse construction is storm safe, which is highly desirable.

Garden Fresh Vegetables uses rock wool insulation for its growing medium. The drip irrigation system along with all other systems are monitored and controlled by a master computer system.

The advantages of hydroponic gardening, according to Fritz, are that there is no soil and no need for chemicals or anything herbicide-related. The disadvantages are that the initial cost of setting up a system on a small scale is somewhat high.

Fritz states that one of the greatest misconceptions about hydroponics is that plants are grown in water. Growing plants in water, he says, is very inefficient. Hydroponics is "grown without soil" not "grown in water."

For those looking to learn about and get into the practice of hydroponics, Fritz reports that it is a very good way to grow produce, because you do not have to use any or very few chemicals. It is "better than organic quality food at commercial prices." It is very unforgiving in applying nutrients, so you must be diligent and have a good system in place to monitor things, but it can produce the best food in the world.

Chapter 5

GROWING MEDIA

Though your plants will get all of their nutrients from the solutions you provide, they still have to have some sort of physical support for their roots. There are many different options for this, some that are organic and some that are man-made. In many cases, there are minimal difference between one type and the next even though many hydroponics gardeners may swear by one medium over another. You might have to do a little trial-and-error research to see what works best for you.

Before making a choice, you will need to know the basic features that a good growing medium should have. Fundamentally, all materials will be light and porous so that they can hold a mix of air and water within them and still allow roots to grow freely between the particles. They also should be chemically inert so that they do not contribute to the nutrient mix that your solution is providing. That would defeat the main purpose of hydroponics.

A selection of materials is listed in the next few sections but there is no limit to what you can work with. If you have access to similar but unlisted materials, feel free to experiment. Also, there are many benefits to mixing two or more of these materials together to get the perfect conditions for your plants.

You will want to consider the absorbency of your medium and what kind of hydroponics you are going to be using. Some systems rely on the medium to *hold* water between pump runs, so you should keep that in mind.

Sand

Sand is a very easily acquired material that is also inexpensive. It has been used as a hydroponic medium, but it is not ideal because the particles are so small that there is little space for air once the water has been added. You can mix sand with perlite or another material to improve the aeration qualities. Once water has been added, sand can be very heavy.

Gravel

This works a lot like sand but with larger particles. Smooth gravel will work better than rough, as it is gentler on your tender, growing roots. The pieces will not absorb any water, so you should not use gravel in any system that requires the medium to store water between irrigations. Ebb and flow is one example where this is not the best option. But any static solution or top-drip system would be fine.

Gravel is quite heavy and would not work well in a raft system. As long as the plant container is supported, you should not have much problem.

You also have to know what kind of rocks are in your gravel. Limestone will have an effect on your water's pH level and should be avoided unless you intend to compensate when you manage your water system.

Vermiculite

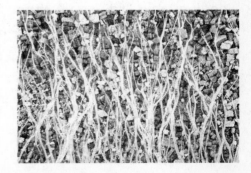

This material is a common addition to potting soil as a way of adding extra absorbency. It is made from mica (a natural mineral) that has been heated until the layers within its structure have burst. This creates a sponge-like particle that works well for this purpose. You will get the best results if you mix vermiculite with another loose material such as perlite because alone it absorbs too much water and has no additional space for air. Roots often will drown if grown in a medium of only vermiculite. A 50/50 blend of vermiculite and perlite works very well.

Vermiculite can be a little dirty to work with as well, because the small pieces can create dust more than the other media. This type of breakdown can start to clog small hoses and filters with fine debris if you are using vermiculite for a long period.

Perlite

This is a similar material to vermiculite but is less absorbent. These particles help create additional air spaces in your medium, which is why it is often mixed with vermiculite or coconut fibre for added drainage capabilities. Perlite particles are harder than vermiculite, so you will not have the same debris or clogging issue with it.

One issue with perlite (and vermiculite as well) is that they are very light and may cause you problems in an ebb-and-flow system if your pots are not held in place or otherwise secured in the flooding table. If they are sitting loose, they likely will start to float as the water level rises during a flood cycle. They may tip over, but the main problem is that the water level will not rise up through the root bundle.

Expanded Clay

This is a very popular medium for larger plants, and it goes by many different brand names like Hydroton®, Geolite and Grow Rocks. It is also sometimes just known as Leca, for lightweight expanded clay aggregate. It is also available in different diameters.

In any case, these are all man-made pellets of very porous clay. They make great support for roots and offer excellent aeration qualities, but they do not hold water on their own. If you need a medium that absorbs and holds water, this is not going to be suitable. But any system with a constant flow of water (most drip arrangements or static solution equipment) will do fine with expanded clay. In many ways, it works a lot like gravel, except that these are much larger pieces and much lighter. Small pots may even be too light, similar to the problems mentioned with perlite.

One of the great benefits of expanded clay is that the pieces are reusable. You can just wash them off between growing projects and use them again with a new set of plants. It is also a good idea to sterilize them gently with a dilute solution of bleach to make sure you are not transferring any mold spores from one growing batch to the next. Being reusable does help to offset the fact that they are more expensive to purchase in the first place. They also should be rinsed off well before their first use to remove any clay dust.

Coconut Fibre

Coconut fibre is becoming one of the more popular types of hydroponic media in use right now, partially because it is inexpensive but it holds water well without smothering roots. It is an all-natural and biodegradable material collected from the outside of coconut shells. It also goes by the name coir or coco peat. The fibre is sold in pressed blocks for easier handling. You have to break it apart before use. It works even better if you add some perlite to the mix for a little extra aeration and drainage.

As with other natural fibres, it can break down over time and constant exposure to water. This will lead to some debris in your water lines that will have to be handled.

Rock Wool

Rock wool is light and very fibrous inorganic material. It is made from heated rock spun into fibres when it is molten. It is pressed into various shapes and sizes to accommodate your hydroponics needs, with small plugs working well for seeds to larger bricks for your more mature plants. Though it is primarily made from natural sources, this inorganic material will not biodegrade.

Loose rock wool can be very dusty, and you should wear a mask if you are going to work around it for very long. Once packed into pots and wet, the dust should cease to be a problem. Working with the pressed forms of this product makes this much less of an issue.

Large-scale growers tend to lean toward rock wool as a medium because its preformed shape is easy to work with, and it has excellent absorption qualities as well. Even though it is a processed product, it is also relatively inexpensive.

Sphagnum Moss

If you prefer working with organic materials, this is another very good option. It is easy to buy at most garden stores as a natural soil additive, and it is not expensive. While moss can be used on its own, it does work better when mixed with sand or perlite to add more air spaces between the pieces. Moss alone is very absorbent and can hold too much water on its own.

Like vermiculite, sphagnum moss will come apart and break down with use and that can be a problem with some hoses and valves. An extra filter on your water system can help a great deal with this.

Oasis Cubes

These are used almost exclusively when starting new cuttings or seeds. Oasis is highly absorbent and will hold water well for tiny developing root hairs. Oasis is a specific brand that is very popular. The cubes are made from an artificial material that is a lot like florist's foam.

They are small squares of foam with a hole for your seed or cutting. You usually buy them in large sheets and just break each cube off as you use it. Once the plants are larger and developing roots, you then transplant the entire piece of foam into a larger portion of whatever main medium you intend on using for the mature plant.

Chapter 6

NUTRIENT SOLUTIONS

You will recall the experiments carried out by Belgian scientist, Jan van Helmont, one of the earliest researchers to record, through scientific method that plants obtain substances such as nutrients from water. Van Helmont planted a five-pound willow shoot in a vessel that contained 200 pounds of dried soil. The vessel was then covered to keep out any possible contaminants. Van Helmont regularly watered the contents of the vessel with rainwater for five years. After this period, he noted that the willow shoot had increased in weight by 160 pounds, but the soil lost less than two ounces. The conclusion that Jan van Helmont drew from this observation was that plants grown in dirt receive their nutrients, not from the dirt, but from the water. It was subsequently realized, at a later date, that plants also benefit from the oxygen and carbon dioxide in the air around them.

John Woodward then, in 1699, determined that pure water was not as good for soil-less plants when compared to water that once had soil soaked in it, which led to the important understanding of how water holds minerals once it has been in contact with soil. This research led to the first man-made nutrient solution for hydroponic gardening.

Now that a wide variety of hydroponic systems have been detailed for you, and you've learned that the primary goal of each of those systems is to deliver nutrients to the plant, we will explore the nature of those nutrients. The liquid nutrient solutions used in hydroponics are the key to having healthy productive plants. It does not matter how expensive or sophisticated your equipment

is, if your nutrients are not done properly, your garden will fail.

This can entail more chemistry than you would like, but all of these upcoming details are important, even if you are going to just buy a jug of solution off the shelf. This is a very important point to underscore. The descriptions of the nutrients defined here might seem overly complicated to those of you that are not proficient in the world of chemistry, but it is good to know that if you gain this understanding of the needs of your plants, it will help you to know what it takes to get the most out of your garden. On the other hand, you also can be comforted by the fact that you can purchase many excellent products that have already figured it out for you. Do whatever works best for you.

As you read through the following information on nutrients and nutrient solutions, recall the information described in Chapter 3 related to water. If you plan to use tap water from your local municipality, you would be well served to understand the chemical make-up of the water you are starting with. Knowing what you are starting with is especially useful if you plan to make your own nutrient solution for your hydroponic system.

If you are using water from a well or of an unknown source (if your water source does not provide a detailed description of your water's composition), you always can take your water in to be tested. You can contact the local health department in your city or county, and they should be able to direct you to a local certified laboratory that will test your water and tell you its exact chemical composition.

Use of Nutrient Solutions

Using nutrient solutions is actually fairly simple. It only gets complicated when you start to create your own nutrient mixes and fine-tune your plants' nutrition.

There are dozens of different brands of solutions for use, all with their own instructions, ratios, and programs. Some are designed to promote flowering, while others are mixed to promote more root growth. Solutions are mixed with water to the proper amounts based on the brand's instructions and then used in your hydroponics system. Some nutrients are one-part, meaning there is just one liquid to mix with water. More in-depth products that allow for more tailoring are two-part or even three-part.

You also will find some fairly basic formulas are purchased as a two-part solution because of potential chemical reactions between ingredients, not because you can (or should) tailor your final solution by adjusting your use of each portion. When in concentrated form, certain compounds will react with each other, causing crystals to form and come out of solution. By diluting each portion first, and then combining, you can avoid these types of reactions. Again, reading the instructions should guide you on how to do this.

Once a solution is measured and used to fill your system's reservoir, you will have to add additional nutrients as time passes and the plants feed from the liquid. This can be tricky since you cannot easily tell how much nutrient compounds remain in the water after it has cycled through your system for several days.

Premixed or Do-It-Yourself Formulas

You can either stick to a premixed or one-part formula to keep things simple or get more creative and start mixing up the individual nutrients yourself to make a custom blend. Needless to say, the first approach is the best one for any hydroponics novice.

The term "do-it-yourself" is a bit of a misnomer, as you will be using commercially made products even if you decide to create your own homemade blend of nutrients. The specific chemicals that go into a typical nutrient solution are outlined later in this chapter, but suffice it to say that it is not something you can put together properly with standard household ingredients.

As mentioned, you will not want to jump into the creation of custom mixes right at the start. But that also does not mean you have to settle for a generic mix either. You can experiment with many specialized formulas. The section at the end of this chapter outlines many of the popular brands and your options for buying solutions.

Electrical Conductivity Measuring

Electrical conductivity measuring is how you determine the mineral content of your solution. Pure water will not conduct electricity. Only dissolved minerals in the water can allow that to happen, so you can measure how many minerals are in the solution based on how well (or how poorly) it conducts electricity.

This measurement will not be able to give you a chemical-by-chemical breakdown of exactly what the water is composed of, but it does provide a very convenient and easy way of quickly determining how nutritionally depleted your reservoir water is. Basically, the more materials that are dissolved in the water, the more electricity it will carry.

Electrical conductivity (EC) is directly measured in milliseimens per centimeter (mS/cm), or also as millimhos per centimeter (mMhos/cm). You will get this reading directly from your meter. Unfortunately, most people are more familiar and more comfortable with parts per million (ppm) as a way of measuring materials in solution. To add to the confusion, other ways of measuring dissolved materials include total dissolved solids (TDS). Because the meter will measure in EC to begin with, that is the most accurate way to describe the nutrient content for hydroponic purposes.

You can make some rough conversions between EC and PPM. A reading of 1 mS/cm can equal anywhere between 500 and 700 ppm depending on whose tables you are checking. The reason why there is no official conversion is because the two units are not really measuring the same thing. Not all materials in solution will have the same EC readings, so there is no way to determine how many parts of anything are in a liquid based solely on the EC readings. These are only approximations. Unfortunately, American gardeners have not adjusted to the use of EC, and most publications still will use ppm references to discuss nutrient concentrations.

With that in mind, most plants do very well with nutrients at a 800 to 1200 ppm level. As you might expect, this will be determined somewhat by the specific nutrient mixture you are using in the first place. Taking EC readings with a fresh batch of solution will give you a baseline to measure subsequent readings against to judge how depleted your mix is becoming over time.

Meters for measuring EC are varied, like with all other hydroponics equipment, and you can adjust your purchase to suit your budget. They fundamentally all work the same way by sensing a small electrical current between two electrodes in the probe. Some meters are meant to be left in the solution at all times and will give you an ongoing reading, and others are just dipped into the water when you want to take a reading.

When measuring EC of your solution, you should habitually take two readings each time. One should be from the solution in your main reservoir, and the other should be taken from within the growing medium of your plants. You do not necessarily have to measure each plant separately, but alternate which ones are being tested with each day's routine. The reason for doing this is to see that the growing medium is not forming a build-up of salts, which would possibly have a negative impact on your plants.

Breakdown of Essential Elements

There are dozens of components in any good nutrient solution, and though you do not need a degree in chemistry to manage your garden, it is a very good idea to understand the basic principles behind these ingredients. Each chemical has a very specific effect on your plants and can be adjusted to create a solution that perfectly suits your gardening needs.

These compounds typically are broken down into two categories: macronutrients and micronutrients. Macronutrients make up the majority of any solution, and they are required in the highest volumes. The micronutrients are necessary but only in smaller trace amounts. Six macronutrients are used in hydroponic solutions: nitrogen, phosphorus, potassium, calcium, magnesium, and sulphur. Each one of these is covered in more detail in this section, and micronutrients will be explained afterwards. Symptoms for both deficiencies and excessive amounts are provided since either one can become a problem in a hydroponic system.

Before continuing, it should be stressed that you do not need to mix and match your own components to create a proper nutrient solution. You can start gardening with any good off-the-shelf blend and not need to know these details to start with. But once your garden is off the ground, almost all hydroponics enthusiasts quickly start experimenting with their ingredients to get that perfect harvest.

Nitrogen (N)

Nitrogen might be considered the most important of all the nutrients, and it influences the vegetative growth of the plant, which means all the leaves and stems. It also is used by the plant in the creation of chlorophyll as well as the proteins used in new cell walls. Because nitrogen is used so much with new growth, you want it to be higher during growth periods before the plant needs to start setting fruit or flowering.

14

N

NITROGEN

7

Because nitrogen is so vital and is used so quickly, it is often part of additional fertilizers as well as standard nutrient solutions. It is provided in two forms in most solutions, as ammonium (NH4) and nitrate (NO3). Ammonium can be too potent for some plants and "burn" them, but nitrate takes longer to be assimilated by the plants cells. A mix of the two can provide a good overall supply of nitrogen.

Deficiency symptoms

Because your plants use it so quickly, nitrogen easily can become deficient in your solution. When the concentrations get too low, the leaves will start to yellow in the spaces between the veins. Lower or older leaves will start to show symptoms first, because nitrogen is a "mobile" nutrient, and plants will move it to newer leaves that need it more. As more leaves turn yellow, they will drop off quickly.

With an interruption in green chlorophyll production, stems and smaller leaves may develop a red or purple cast to them (usually the underside of the leaf rather than the top surface).

Excessive nitrogen symptoms

At first, it will seem as though your plants are vigorously thriving by producing a large number of new leaves. But you soon will notice that the stems are weak, and the leaves will be bent over as they grow. Any flowers that bloom will be small with overly fine petals. After a short time, leaves will start to turn brown, dry out, and fall off. If you check the roots, they will be very slow to grow as the plant is putting all its energy into developing excessive foliage.

Phosphorus (P)

While nitrogen is used in leaf production, phosphorus is most notably involved in flowering, fruiting and seed production. It also is used heavily by plants at the early stages of germination and seedling growth. Most nutrient solutions geared toward improved blooms or fruit production are high in phosphorus. Chemically, it is used in many plant enzymes, and it is a compound in DNA.

Deficiency symptoms

Overall growth of your plants will be stunted, particularly any flowering that should be taking place. Any blooms that do come out will be smaller than usual. Some of the first signs of low phosphorus will be in the leaves. Veins will start to darken, turning purplish or black. The parts of the leaves between the veins also will start to turn black, starting at the tip of the leaf and slowly taking over the whole leaf at which point it usually drops off.

You also can get phosphorus deficiency symptoms if your plants are lacking in zinc (a micronutrient) because zinc is necessary for the plant to properly use its phosphorus supply. Phosphorus uptake also can be interrupted if your solution has a pH over 7. These are two other areas you should always check on when you see plants with deficiency symptoms that are not improved with added phosphorus.

Excessive phosphorus symptoms

Having too much phosphorus in your system usually will not create too many negative symptoms because the plants can handle this element, even in high concentrations. It will start to interfere with the use of other nutrients, so having too much phosphorus can manifest as a deficiency in other minerals (such as calcium, zinc, magnesium, and copper).

Potassium (K)

Potassium is used in all forms of plant growth, and it helps the plant handle production of sugars and starches. High potassium levels also encourage sturdy root growth and can help plants resist fungal attacks.

39

K

POTASSIUM

19

Deficiency Symptoms

When your solution starts to run low in potassium, your plants will start to yellow (older leaves will show symptoms first). The yellowing tends to take place across the entire leaf surface when it first starts. The leaves will start to dry around the edges, showing brown crisp tips at the ends. Larger patches of rust-brown can start to show up on the rest of the leaf before they drop off. If you are growing flowering plants, they likely will fail to bloom.

Most leaves will start to look dull on the surface and lose their natural shine.

Excessive potassium symptoms

As with phosphorus, having too much potassium usually will lead to a reduction in other minerals such as magnesium, zinc, and iron. There are no specific symptoms that would lead you to a diagnosis of excessive potassium.

The previous three macronutrients are considered primary nutrients because they are so fundamental in a plant's growth and development. The next three are considered secondary, though they are just as vital to overall plant health.

Calcium (Ca)

Calcium is used by the plant in creating new cell walls; particularly in the fast-growing root tip zones.

Deficiency symptoms

Stems can start to weaken, creating a droopy look as the stems are unable to hold up the leaves completely. Unlike the typical yellowing that occurs with many other nutrient deficiencies, a lack of calcium will create very dark leaves. Younger leaves will show symptoms before the older ones because calcium does not transport well through the plant.

Very new leaves will start to turn yellow as the problem persists, and can even turn dark purple. Overall growth of the plant will be reduced, or stopped altogether.

Excessive calcium symptoms

Too much calcium in your nutrient solution is not going to cause many symptoms though your plants can start to wilt if it gets too high. It also can be evident in your solution reservoir as it can cloud the water.

Magnesium (Mg)

Magnesium is one of the chemical components of chlorophyll, and it will be used in large amounts in fast-growing plants (annuals). You should not confuse this with manganese, which is still important but as a micronutrient only.

Deficiency symptoms

This is one of the more common problems you will find with nutrient deficiencies in hydroponics plants. Unfortunately, it also can take a few weeks before symptoms start to develop. Lower leaves will start to yellow, which quickly spreads across the entire leaf. The leaves will turn extremely yellow or even off-white before they finally die and drop off the plant. As it progresses, the edges of the leaves will start to dry and brown, and rusty spots can start to form on the leaf.

Even if your solution has the proper levels of magnesium, it may not be taken up by the plants if the roots are being kept too cool. Raise the temperature and see if that improves the situation.

Excessive magnesium symptoms

Having an excess of magnesium is not going to cause any particular problems, and you will not see any adverse symptoms in your plants if this happens.

Sulfur (S)

Many plant processes involve sulfur, particularly the creation of vitamins and hormones necessary for plant development. Calcium will bond with sulphur to create calcium sulphate (also known as gypsum), and it can cloud the water or even settle out as a solid. This can lead to a lack of sulphur in solution, creating a deficiency.

Deficiency symptoms

As usual, you will be looking for yellowed leaves though the progression is a little different than with the other elements. The newer leaves will start to show their symptoms first, and usually at their base rather than the tips. The veins usually stay deep green with the rest of the leaf getting paler as the problem persists. Eventually, the leaf tips will curl downward and may show some signs of burning or drying at the edges. There will not be any brown spots across the leaf but some stems can start to look dark and purplish.

Excessive sulphur symptoms

Your plants will not suffer dramatically if there is a high level of sulphur in their solution though overall growth will be slow and leaves will be darker green than usual.

Micronutrients

That covers the main six nutrients that will go into your growing solutions. Now comes the collection of elements that are found in very small trace amounts but are nonetheless still important to proper plant growth. Just because a plant does not need large amounts of any compound does not make it dispensable. Unlike the details given for the six macronutrients, only a short mention will be made of the deficiency symptoms for each one.

Zinc (Zn)

Crucial for creation of chlorophyll and other enzymes, zinc is often found to be deficient in soil-grown plants though most nutrient solutions have an adequate supply. A lack of zinc will lead to yellowing of the leaves with some browning along the edges. It is similar in appearance to magnesium deficiency, but without the spots of brown on the leaf surface. New leaves will have a crinkled appearance or look otherwise deformed. The same goes for flowers. Overall plant growth is very slow when there is a low level of zinc.

Iron (Fe)

Plants do not absorb iron easily, so you need to have a good concentration of it available in your solution to ward off deficiencies. Acid solutions also will inhibit iron uptake, so check on your pH if you detect a problem. Younger leaves show symptoms first because iron is not easily moved around the plant and cannot be drawn from older leaves for use. The spaces between the veins will start to yellow, starting at the base of the leaf. The veins usually remain green.

Manganese (Mn)

Do not confuse this element with the macronutrient magnesium, though their deficiency symptoms are actually very similar. The veins remain green while the rest of the leaf slowly turns yellow, starting around the base of the leaf. Dead patches can start to form, which are not the same as the discolored brown or rust patches found with some other deficiency issues. Overall plant growth is stunted, and the plant will take a long time to mature.

The following micronutrients are important but required in such small quantities that it is seldom a problem. You only likely will find deficiencies in these if you are experimenting with your own personal nutrient solutions rather than using a commercial blend. Even so, a good gardener is always familiar with all potential problems.

Chlorine (Cl)

Considering that chlorine is added to almost all municipal water supplies, it is highly unlikely that you will find a deficiency even if you are filtering your water. Roots will develop improperly, leaving them very short and leaves will take on an unusual bronze color. Since it is a typical water additive, it is one of the few elements that you can run a risk of excess. Young leaves quickly will have dead or burned edges that eventually will spread through the plant if you do not fix the problem.

Copper (Cu)

Younger leaves will wilt and turn a brownish-gray if there is not enough copper in your solution. The wilting will spread to the whole plant, and you can use a copper-based fungicide to add some additional copper as a quick treatment. Excessive copper will lead to a darkening of the roots and slow growing plants. If your solution is acidic, it can make a copper overdose worse. Copper is required in very small amounts, so you do need to be careful not to overdo your treatment.

Nickel (Ni)

It is very unlikely you ever will come across a nickel deficiency, and there are no unique symptoms you will be able to identify.

Boron (B)

A lack of boron will give your plants stubby roots, and new leaves quickly will become burned looking right after they emerge. As the deficiency continues, the darkening or burning of leaves will move down the plant to impact older leaves. There can be wilting and the formation of dead or rotting spots in your leaves.

Silicon (Si)

It is believed that a deficiency in silicon can cause plants to stop producing new leaves or simply have a lower level of productivity. It is a very common element in water, and specific studies into its purpose have not been done.

Sodium (Na)

This refers to the pure element of sodium, not the sodium chloride we are used to as table salt. Sodium is one element you do not want to have if you can avoid it, and the water you use to mix up your nutrient solution should have no more than 50 ppm in concentration.

Chelates

This refers to a type of format that micronutrients can be in, rather than a specific type of nutrient itself. Since you often will see it on product labels, it bears mentioning. Micronutrients tend to bond with other compounds in a fertilizer, making them less effective when used in a hydroponic solution. Those that have been chemically treated to give them a protective coating are said to be chelated, and they are a better choice for your plants. Amino acid chelates are the best, with glycine chelates coming a close second. Cheaper solutions will have chelates created with EDTA that will eventually become toxic to your plants if you use the product over a long period.

Nutrient Composition Values

Though you cannot use an EC meter to measure each component in your solution, it can be helpful to have a reference table of concentrations for each element. When working with separate products or blending your own fertilizers, you will need to have a rough awareness of how much each nutrient should be.

The following list provides the average amounts you will want in ppm for each major nutrient in a solution. These are just estimates, and your plants can tolerate wider ranges.

Nitrogen	250 ppm
Phosphorus	80 ppm
Potassium	300 ppm
Calcium	200 ppm
Magnesium	75 ppm
Sulfur	400 ppm
Iron	5 ppm
Copper	0.05 ppm
Zinc	0.5 ppm
Boron	1 ppm
Manganese	2 ppm

As mentioned, your standard EC measurements will not provide this detail to you. But other chemical test kits can provide a better look at the concentrations of each element in a solution. Garden stores offer great kits you can use to test for specific elements, though this is not something you will want to deal with on a daily basis as you would with an EC reading. But when creating new fertilizer blends or trying a new product, taking the time to do a little testing can help you see what you are working with.

Handling Imbalances

As you can see from the above section, there can be a whole list of potential problems with your plants if one or more of these nutrients are in the wrong amount. Deficiencies are more common than excesses since plants simply cease drawing in certain chemicals once they no longer need them. Of course, this is not a perfect system, and you can have some toxic symptoms if certain chemicals are in too high concentrations.

But the issue is that you do not manage your nutrient solution one chemical at a time. The fact that you are low in sulphur or potassium does not simply mean you add more of it to the batch. This is especially true if you are using a premixed liquid formulation for your garden.

Once you start seeing deficiencies in your plants, you will want to take some EC readings and likely start a new batch of solution in the reservoir if it has become too dilute. If your EC figures indicate that the overall batch is still nutrient-rich, then you need to focus on the chemical you are lacking.

If you consistently have growth problems with your plants, you need to change solutions completely. With so many brands and mixtures on the market, there is no reason to assume that they are all the same. Each one will have a little variation with its formula, so look around to find one that is higher in whatever element you are frequently short of. Or use other additives to boost that one element in your mixture. The next section covers fertilizers that can be used as additions to your regular nutrient solution mix in order to modify the chemical make-up.

Flushing

Though excesses are less common than deficiencies, they also can be a little harder to treat because they can build up in the growing medium and require that you flush them out. When your plants start showing symptoms of toxic element buildup but the solution itself is not high in concentration (based on your EC readings), you can assume that these compounds have accu-mulated in the growing medium. Products such as XNutrients's Flushing Solution or Botanicare's® Clearex™ are both designed for this purpose. Plain water also will work if you prefer to keep things simple.

Replace your nutrient solution with either water or one of the clearing products, and measure the EC before you begin. Run it through your system for a few cycles (depending on the type of system you are working). Measure the EC again, and it should be higher as the minerals come out of the growing medium. Do this a few more times until you stop seeing an increase with each flushing. Then empty out the reservoir again, and go back to your regular nutrient solution.

Fertilizers

This section will include a number of compounds and chemicals used in addition to your standard nutrient solutions rather than on their own. Some can be used to correct nutrient deficiencies, and some simply are used as additives to help your plants thrive.

Many brands of additives and fertilizers are on the market, far more than could be listed here. Most of them are just variations on the basic nutrient solution, and you can find out more about this later in this chapter. But you also can use more natural materials to increase certain elements in your solutions if you want a simpler (and often cheaper) approach.

Natural Compounds

If you are going the natural route, here are some of the more common additives you can use in your hydroponic garden. They usually are intended for soil-gardening use, which means you will have to do a little more work to use them in a liquid-only scenario. You will save money with most of these compared to purchased fertilizers, though you will lose the precisely measured contents that a commercial product offers. The route you choose is up to you.

Another benefit to using these materials is that you can add just one or two elements to your mix by using them. Purchased solutions usually are made up of many components, which may not suit your needs.

For the most part, these products are all sold as solids and will need to be turned into a format you can use in a hydroponic nutrient solution. Depending on the material, that can be as simple as letting some of the solids soak in water in order to extract the elements. This is a very imprecise method, and if you are going to do this, it would be a good idea to invest in some chemical test kits (sold in gardening stores) to test the solutions you create.

Epsom salts

This is the common name for magnesium sulphate, which can be used to add both magnesium as well as sulphur to your solutions. You do need to purchase agricultural grade salt though, not the type used for bath water. As a salt, it does dissolve very easily in water, so you should have no trouble creating a solution with it. Start with ¼ teaspoon per gallon of solution for the additional elements. A similar dilute mixture actually can be sprayed on the leaves to provide magnesium to the plant.

Lime

Sometimes known as dolomite lime or just dolomite, this material is a great source of additional calcium, and it also can help to balance out pH problems. It should dissolve in water well enough to make a solution, and you should start with ½ teaspoon per gallon of water to create a calcium-rich mixture.

Animal manures

Manure can come from a number of different animals, each with a subtle difference from the other. Overall, manure will be high in nitrogen, phosphorus, and potassium, which makes it an ideal fertilizer because it provides the three primary macronutrients together. Buying aged manure is easy enough at the garden store, but if you have access to fresh material, you need to wait at least three months before using it. It will be too high in nitrogen when fresh. Soak some dry manure in water to create a fertilizer-rich liquid that will work well in your solutions.

Potash

This is better known as wood ash (though that is not the only source) and an excellent source of potassium. You can use the powdered form or buy potash liquid supplements that may work better in a hydroponic system. Care needs to be taken as potash is extremely basic (a pH level close to 10 or more), so using this as a potassium supplement needs to be done in conjunction with other components to lower the pH levels. It affects pH so strongly that you also could use potash for that reason alone if your solutions are too acidic.

Seaweed

This is a commonly found fertilizer for soils, made up of dried seaweed that has been mashed into a rough powder. Many species of seaweed may be used, but kelp is the most common ingredient in seaweed-based products. Like potash, this is a good source of potassium as well as a mix of other trace elements.

Coffee grounds

You would not want to use
actual brewed coffee as it
would be far too strong as a
nutrient fertilizer, but if you
soak *used* grounds in water,

you can make a much more dilute and suitable solution. You can
use this as a way to add nitrogen or also to lower the pH because
it is notably acidic.

Fish emulsion

Fish emulsion is a liquid product made from fish, and it makes
a good fertilizer that works well in hydroponics due to its liquid state. You can buy a powdered form (called fish meal), which
has mainly the same contents but will be harder to work with. It
is high in nitrogen and phosphorus, though it will have a very
strong and unpleasant odor.

Bone meal

You can find bone meal in most garden stores as a powdered form
of animal bones. Like with other animal products, this will provide a rich source of nitrogen and phosphorus. It comes in various forms, including raw or steamed. The raw will have slightly
more nitrogen, but the steamed meal is usually a finer powder,
which will work better to create a liquid solution.

Blood meal

Nitrogen is the main element you get from using dried blood meal
(again, easily found in any garden supply store). It will need to
be soaked in order to create a liquid solution you can work with.

Foliar sprays

On the topic of fertilizers, you should know that not all products are used in solutions for the roots to absorb. You can take another route and provide many important nutrients through the leaves instead. Called foliar sprays, many soluble nutrients can be taken up through pores in the leaves, which means you can directly add certain fertilizers without altering the main nutrient your system is using.

The natural shiny or waxy surface of most leaves can make this a challenge. There are products on the market that will help make the surface "stickier" to other fluids and should be used in combination with foliar fertilizer sprays. Earth Juice Assist™ is one good agent that should be used before you start fertilizing the leaves by spraying.

Unlike the roots, which are designed to take in most of the plants nutrients, the leaves are not so adept at it. Keep all fertilizer sprays dilute, no more than 500 ppm of whatever nutrient you are using. This should only be a short-term solution to a nutrient problem and not part of your daily routine. You should be relying on foliar spraying no more than once a week. If your plants require certain nutrients more than that, you should adjust their nutrient solution instead and let the roots do the work, as they are meant to.

Other Additives

So far this section has covered a number of standard chemical nutrients and fertilizers that provide additional nutrients to your plants. But several other possible additives you can have in your solutions can be beneficial to your plants, though not from a strictly nutrition standpoint.

Vitamin C

Also known chemically as ascorbic acid, there is some debate on the usefulness of adding it to a nutrient solution for hydroponic plants. Those who use it will add it to their solutions right near blooming or harvest time, often mixed with molasses or sugar for an added nutrient boost. Since plants do manufacture their own sugars as well as vitamin C, this may not be that helpful. But some do swear by it, so you always can consider it an option for some experimentation. Big Bud® is one commercial product that touts ascorbic acid as a great additive for improved flowering.

Ethylene gas

This one is a little different, as it is a gas rather than a liquid. Ethylene is produced by some kinds of fruit (mostly apples) as they ripen, and it prompts a ripening or maturation response in other nearby plants as well. You can introduce the gas in your growing room to help speed-up maturation and fruit development of your plants or to induce early flowering. This is not easily purchased, and you may have better luck creating your own with a few baskets of ripe apples left in your growing area.

Plant hormones

This actually includes a large number of compounds. Auxins, cytokinins, and gibberellins are the most commonly used in hydroponic fertilizers. These chemicals are used by the plants as triggers to encourage further growth, with the details depending on the hormone. Hormones usually are mixed in with other nutrients in fertilizers rather than being available on their own.

American Hydroponics has one mix of nutrients called Supernova™ that is high in hormones, particularly cytokinins.

Humic acid and fulvic acid

Both compounds are extracted from organic compost, and they can help with plant growth, leaf formation, and keep your plants strong. Many other additives are mixed with humic or fulvic acid as a base for the formula, but you also can buy products that are strictly these acids as an additive themselves.

Mycorrhyzia

Plant roots can benefit from helpful fungus called mycorrhyzia, which helps extract additional nutrients from your solutions. These additives increase root strength and generally provide a healthier environment for your roots to develop. Most products with mycorrhyzia also include a mix of other beneficial bacteria to create a complete natural ecosystem for your roots.

Sugar and molasses

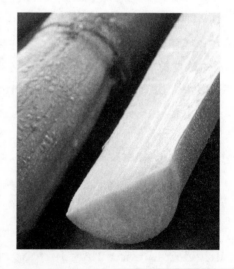

This was mentioned above with vitamin C, and bears mentioning again on its own as a nutrient additive. Plants are able to produce their own sugars, so they will do just fine without any additions in this area. You can add sugar to a solution in the form of simple sugar as well as molasses or honey. It can stimulate additional growth and can help reduce the instance of fungus in the roots (particularly when you use honey).

Commercial Products

Though there are too many specific types of nutrient products to list accurately, here are some of the common ones that are good for most garden types and beginner setups. Many of these are complete solutions that would be used on their own in your system, but some are additions that you would use at certain times in the season or to counteract certain nutritional problems.

For the most part, hydroponic solutions are very complex and products are not simply offered with one or two minerals as ingredients. If you need *only* potassium, you will have to either work with potash on your own or replace your existing solution with a brand with a higher potassium content. It is not likely you will be able to buy a fertilizer that is *just* potassium. Most blends will include standard nutrients (in a mix of amounts and ratios) as well as other compounds like those listed above in the Additives section. They often have their own proprietary mix of amino acids, vitamins, hormones, and more that are not explicitly listed. Prepare for some trial and error once you go beyond the very basic mixes.

One further note on nutrients and fertilizers is the notation of three numbers included with most products that have a broad nutrient composition (as opposed to those that are just fertilizers or additives). These figures represent the nitrogen-phosphorus-potassium (N-P-K) content, and will make your label reading a little easier if you are focusing on these main nutrients. For example, the popular FloraGro solution by General Hydroponics® reads 2-1-6, meaning that it contains 2 percent nitrogen, 1 percent phosphorus and 6 percent potassium.

General Hydroponics

This is a popular line of hydroponics solutions, and their Flora series is one of the most popular solutions that work as a general standard formula. This is a very good place to start if you are looking for your first solution. There are three blends: FloraGro for general plant growth, FloraBloom for flowering or fruiting periods, and FloraMicro has a mix of the micronutrients. They also have another three-part line called Floralicious that focuses on organic and vegan ingredients but offers the same concept of growth, flowering, and micronutrients. They also carry other fertilizers and supplements.

Botanicare™

You also can get very good basic solutions from Botanicare, and their Pure Blend® line is similar to the products just mentioned above. Each is a one-part liquid solution, and there is one formula for general plant growth and one for blooms and fruit. There is also an additional one specific to soil growing or coco fiber. If you are looking for base solutions, their Triflex and CNS17 lines offer some other N-P-K blends to choose from. Each one has a simple growth formula as well as one for flowers and fruit production. Botanicare also has a selection of more specialized fertilizers and amendments that you can use to fine-tune your overall system. They have a fulvic acid solution and a blend made with organic seaweed emulsions.

Fox Farm®

Fox Farm sells many kinds of fertilizers, including some for soil growing as well as hydroponics. Make sure you know which you are buying. They have two very good products for hydroponics use. Their Grow Big® mixture makes a good all-around nutrient solution, and the Big Bloom mix is unusually mild and makes a good choice when you need to flush out your system if you have nutrient imbalances built up.

Earth Juice™

You can get good base solutions from Earth Juice, focusing on standard growth or flowering stages and they also have a nutrient booster called Catalyst that has a mixture of molasses and kelp emulsions for a little extra help. They also carry pH adjusters and a potassium-based fertilizer called Earth Juice Meta to improve harvesting production. Earth Juice also offers root stimulators and cloning products for when you are propagating new plants.

Advanced Nutrients®

Most of their products are more expensive than the others, but you will find a huge selection of formulas and mixes for your plants with Advanced Nutrients. Their basic line comes in three formulas: Grow, Bloom and Micro, which are similar to other products already mentioned. They also have more sophisticated products that come in two parts to be mixed after you dilute them. Their Connoisseur and Sensei Grow solutions are both two-part mixtures. Some of their products are fancifully named, such as Voodoo Juice, Hammerhead, and Wet Betty. But if you take the time to read the ingredients, you probably will find just about any type of formula you could want. They also have several pH adjusters for when your levels are out of line.

Roots Organics

Roots Organics have a mix of products, but their Soul Synthetics make a great base for your nutrient needs. They do use synthetic compounds rather than natural ones, so you will have to be the judge of that. You can get the typical grow and flower blends, as well as mixes with micronutrients, extra amino acids, or other custom combinations to suit any situation. They lean towards flowering boosters, though you definitely can get some benefits for fruiting plants, too.

Humbolt Nutrients

Like the others, Humbolt has a three-part baseline of nutrients that favor basic plant growth, flowering, and micronutrient fertilizers. But they have a number of more unique products to their name as well. Their list of products includes additives such as humic acid, seaweed emulsions and honey-based carbohydrates, and a mycorrhizal root treatment.

ENVIRONMENTAL CONTROL

*U*p to this point we have concerned ourselves with the plant, the system that feeds the plant, and the nutrient that the plant is fed. The plant and the system, however, do not exist in a vacuum. The environment that the system exists in is every bit as important as the medium in which the plant anchors its roots. The air temperature, humidity, flow, light, and several other environmental factors all contribute to the quality of life that effect your plants. Hydroponic gardeners simply do not set their gardens up on the kitchen table and watch their plants grow. While this is certainly an option, most will go the extra step to further provide the right conditions for their indoor gardens. That includes lighting, air control, and more. How sophisticated you wish to be is up to you.

Lights

If you are running a hydroponic system in an outdoor greenhouse, you may be able to rely on natural lighting for your plants. In any indoor case, you will have to provide lights. Unfortunately, this can be nearly as complicated as your water system itself because you need to provide light that is as close to sunlight as possible. Your average room lights will not be sufficient. Before any further discussion on lighting options, you need to know more about the properties of light.

Understanding light intensity

When it comes to measuring light, most people think of watts. A standard incandescent light bulb was between 60 and 100 watts before the advent of compact fluorescent bulbs. Now a "standard" bulb is about 23 watts when using CFLs. Many people use the term to describe how bright a light is even though that is not really what watts measure. Watts is a term used to measure energy or power.

True brightness or intensity can be measured with various units such as lumens and lux. Lumens, known in other terms as luminous flux, measure the perceived power of light from a natural or artificial light source. Simply put, lumens measure of how bright a light source is, not taking distance into account.

Lux is the measurement of the apparent intensity of light at a given distance. A light source ten feet away will have a far greater lux than if you were 100 feet away.

Nonetheless, most light bulbs are sold with wattage ratings rather than lumens or lux, so that is still likely the information you are going to have to work with when you are shopping for lights, though it is well worth your while to know the definitions of each of these terms and how they apply to your situation. As a point of comparison, a typical 23-watt household light bulb will put out approximately 1,500 lumens. A 125-watt bulb will produce 9500 lumens.

Understanding the color spectrum

Many people are familiar with wattage, but understanding the color in light is usually a new concept. It is a very important one though. Even very subtle color components can impact your plants.

Lights that lean to the red end of the spectrum will promote flowering and fruiting, and lights with more blue will encourage faster overall growth and leaf production. Sometimes these lights are known as warm and cool, respectively. Since you are in control of your lighting, you can make bulb choices that favor your growing needs. Herbs and leafy plants will do better with cool lights, and most other plants will produce better under warm. And sometimes, combinations of each type will work to your advantage as well.

Kinds of lighting options

Even something as simple as a light bulb is going to come in several varieties. There are actually many different kinds, and they all may or may not have a place in a hydroponic system.

Household incandescent bulbs are not very good for several reasons. They do not provide the proper spectrum of light, and they are extremely hot compared to fluorescent bulbs. In an enclosed area, heat is very important and will be a detriment to your gardening. Not to mention the short life span of an incandescent bulb. Considering your lights will be on for most of the day, every day, you will spend a lot of time replacing bulbs if you use incandescent bulbs.

Primarily, two kinds of lights are used in hydroponics, though lighting is currently going through a great deal of change. High pressure sodium and metal halide have been the lights of choice for gardeners in the recent past. Both are considered high intensity discharge (HID) lighting. While these are the better quality lights intended to be used as grow lights, small hydroponics setups can be very successful with regular room-lighting fluorescents as long as you get them large enough and bright enough for your plants. Here are the basic points about each type of lamp, without going into the chemistry that makes one different from the other.

High-pressure sodium (HPS) bulbs have more light in the red end of the spectrum, with metal halide (MH) bulbs leaning the other way to the blue end. Overall though, MH lights offer a wider spectrum of light and are closer to natural sunlight in terms of the color content. Large hydroponic operations often combine the two in order to create the most complete possible spectrum. Most home gardeners will not have the space or the budget to manage two different sets of lights, so you will have to make a choice. MH lights are the more practical choice for most indoor gardening situations but if you have a setup that does get a significant amount of natural sunlight already, then you can use HPS as a supplement.

Both types of bulbs are offered on the market in a range of wattages, running from 150-watt to more than 1000-watt. Costs are comparable, though MH lights can be more costly at the higher wattages. That also will depend on the manufacturer, as some are more expensive than others.

LED lights (light emitting diode) seem to be the wave of the future of lighting. LEDs last much longer than anything currently on the market and will give the gardener the ease and ability to offer plants the specific colors necessary for each stage of growth. LEDs allow the hydroponic gardener the ability to create custom wavelength combinations for their plants to adjust the photosynthesis and/or photomorphogenesis responses of the intended plant. With LED lighting, the hydroponic gardener can tailor the lighting to the ideal needs of specific plant species. By combining customized wavelength combinations with easily changed LED lights and light fixtures, the hydroponic gardener can change the photosynthesis and/or photomorphogenesis response of the specified plant, allowing more vigorous growth in shorter periods.

While LEDs are currently somewhat more expensive than other forms of lighting options, the hydroponic gardener will find that, in the long run, they are less expensive to maintain. The lights are also much cheaper to operate than anything currently on the market. Determining precisely what your cheapest lighting option is can be a bit of a complicated science, as you need to go beyond the cost of the lighting equipment and the cost of powering the lights. You also need to consider the results generated by the lights. At the end of the day, LEDs seem to lead the pack and are well worth your further exploration.

The use of LEDs for growth operations is a brand new field at the time of this writing, but it is well worth any indoor gardener's time and effort to stay current on this topic. LEDs have been available to the home gardener for only about three to four years.

Ballasts

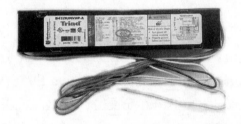

The above section has dealt with bulbs and the components of lighting that actually produce light, but lighting has more to it than that. Fluorescent bulbs (either HPS or MH), incandescent lights, and LEDs all will require the proper sockets and fittings in order to use them. They are called ballasts, and the ballasts needed for each kind of light source varies with the lighting option you choose.

Ballasts contain capacitors and transformers to manage the power coming into your lights, and they also are designed to dissipate the heat build-up that comes with running lights. They are rated for different wattages, so you need to plan your purchase based on the lights you plan to use. If you are just starting out, you should get a complete lighting kit that includes all the bulbs, sockets, ballasts, and even a reflector all in one purchase, so that you know everything works properly together.

The ballast is housed in a small box, which either can be installed directly to the light bulb or left on a nearby flat surface and attached to the light with the appropriate cord. Each ballast usually has an on/off switch and can be controlled by a separate timer if you are going to have your lights operate automatically.

Light placement

Now comes the more important information about how to determine how many lights you need and how you should arrange them for maximum efficiency. The following information is related to the use of incandescent lighting. The use of LEDs requires much less energy.

A very rough estimate of lighting needs is 40 to 75 watts per square foot of growing area. So a 1200-watt light fixture could supply light for at least 30 square feet of plant space. This is a place to start with your calculations, but it is not the final figure. How high you hang your lights also will come into play. Your lights will have to be adjustable so you can raise them up as your plants grow. Chains are the best option for this since you can hang your lights on hooks, and then just change which links are used to move the light up or down.

Having the precise position of your lights for optimum growth is a nice idea, but it is not an easy one to achieve for the novice. This is where you need to do some work figuring out lumens and lux based on the wattage of your lights. You also should have a good light meter on hand to help you measure the light accurately, so you are not guessing about intensity or distance.

Reflectors

The lights themselves are only part of the system. To make your lighting arrangement as efficient as possible, you want to have a little more control over how the light is cast over your plants. The main way to do this is with a reflector.

Though there are different varieties and styles on the market, all reflectors are basically the same concept. A reflective hood is attached over the light bulb so that light is not wasted by shining it upward, away from the plants. Light is reflected down where the plants are. Using a reflector will bring more light to your plants, more so than what the initial wattage rating would indicate. So if

you are going to install reflectors over your lights, you should use a light meter at plant-level to see precisely how much light is going to be used by your plants.

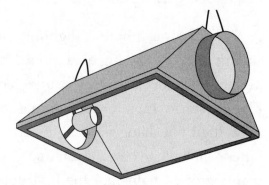

LEDs, generally, do not require reflectors, as the lights are precisely directional to begin with. One of the strengths of LED lighting is that there is not much spillage, and very little light is wasted in dispersal.

Light movers

Reflectors are probably obvious and are a very logical addition to your light fixtures. But you can add another level of control by using movers. These are not strictly necessary and most beginners will not want to use them due to their cost.

A light mover is a powered track that allows your light fixtures to move, usually from one side of the room to the other. The purpose is to mimic the natural movement that would happen with sunlight and to allow more of your plants to get the full effect from each light. If you were to have one single fixture over your plants, you would be able to provide its full effect across the entire growing table if the light shifted positions through the day. It may be a reasonable alternative to buying a second light and ballast.

Temperature

After lighting, you will want to turn your attention to the temperature of your growing area. You need to keep the area warm enough for your plants to thrive but prevent it from overheating (which can happen due to the lights and other constantly running power equipment).

There is no optimum temperature that will suit all plants, so you will have to choose a comfortable range for everything you are growing. Most plants will be happy at 75 degrees F during the day with a drop to 60 degrees F at night. A cooling period at night is necessary, so do not plan on keeping a static heat level 24 hours a day. If you are growing plants that are only going to thrive in cool weather (lettuce is a good example), then try to keep it cooler by around 10 degrees.

If your ambient home temperature does not suit this, you will have to add heat to your grow room. Seventy-five degrees is a little warm for most people. Before you start buying room heaters, see how much added heat the lights give off. Your grow room might maintain the proper temperature naturally after all. If you have a large setup, your lights may produce more heat than you want, even with active fans and exhaust venting. In that case, you may have to get a small room air conditioner to keep the overall temperature in the right zone.

CO_2 Gas Supplementation

This is going to be a more advanced concept and not something for the novice to be concerned about at the start. Plants are living things that require oxygen (O_2) to survive just as we do, but they also need carbon dioxide (CO_2) to run their photosynthesis. They naturally produce CO_2 on their own, but you can give them a boost by adding extra to their atmosphere.

Typical room atmosphere will have about 300 ppm (parts per million) CO_2. Plants will start to show the most benefit from it when the levels reach at least 1000 ppm. You definitely will need to get a meter to measure the levels, so you do not over-gas your plants. We will learn more on carbon dioxide meters in the next section of this chapter.

Commercial operations routinely use additional CO_2, and they report that it can boost overall productivity by up to 20 percent. Whether that justifies the additional effort and equipment costs is up to you. It also will require that you have an enclosed area for your setup to keep the gas contained.

There are two common methods for adding carbon dioxide to the environment. The first is the use of bottled pressurized gas. Using a control valve on the bottle and air hoses to deliver the gas to your plants, you can boost the overall CO_2 levels. These types of gas bottles are large, heavy and get expensive to have refilled, so this is not an ideal option. It may be a decent approach to first try the technique and see if your plants benefit. If it is something you want to consider, then you can take it a step further with a proper CO_2 generator.

These generators produce carbon dioxide by burning natural gas or propane, by means of a burner and pilot light. Green Air Products makes some popular models of carbon dioxide generators that work well in hydroponics, and they will cost a few hundred dollars each.

They also produce heat, which may be a positive or negative for your system. If you already need a little extra heat for your plants, this would be a good way to do that without adding a heater as well. Otherwise, you will need to watch the temperature carefully and allow for fans and venting to release the added heat. Since heat rises and CO_2 falls, a vent that is higher on the walls or the roof will help let out the heat without letting out the CO_2 you are trying to accumulate.

Carbon dioxide enrichment will only help your plants while the lights are running and the plants are actively photosynthesizing. Whatever method you are using to produce CO_2 can be shut off at night without any detrimental effect on your plants.

When using any type of CO_2 enrichment, you will need to have a fan or two in place as well to keep the gas moving in the area. Carbon dioxide is heavier than oxygen, and it will sink if left on its own. Hoses that deliver gas directly to the plants will help overcome this if you are using bottled gas.

When you boost your plants' metabolisms, you will find that they start to draw more heavily on other resources as well. Any previously adequate levels of water and nutrient likely will be insufficient once the carbon dioxide starts to take effect.

Also, keep in mind that CO_2 will be toxic to you and your family if levels rise too high in the rest of your home. Take proper measures to keep your carbon dioxide additions limited to your grow area, and keep a good monitor (with alarm) to let you know if it starts to leak into the rest of your home.

Meters

With all these variables, you will need to plan to have some meters to measure your hydroponic environment. There are several that will come in handy when you are setting up your grow room.

Thermometers

This one, used to measure the temperature of your grow space, is fairly simple and straightforward. As mentioned in the temperature section above, you have to take care not to let your space overheat from all the lights. Any standard thermometer can help you keep track, though a digital one can be easier to read than the old-fashioned "mercury" style.

A thermostat can trigger fans and heaters to help maintain a steady temperature in your growing area.

Hygrometers

A hygrometer measures the humidity in the air. High humidity is an inevitable result of all the flowing water and liquid in hydroponics, which is usually quite fine as plants like having a lot of moisture around. Like with any factor, you can have too much of it. If there is too much moisture in the air, your

plants will not be able to breathe properly or take in new liquid (and therefore nutrients) through their roots. You will want to aim for between 65 and 70 percent humidity for most plants, though flowers can do better with 55 to 60 percent.

Since adding humidity is rarely necessary, it has not yet been discussed as an atmospheric requirement. You can up the humidity in your grow room by adding some open buckets of wet sand. A proper humidifier also can work if you do not mind yet another piece of equipment running. If you do have excess moisture, you just have to run a dehumidifier or add additional venting to the room to remove the wet air. You also could look at your nutrient solution systems to see if you can reduce any unnecessary evaporation.

Carbon dioxide monitors

This is not as crucial as the other two unless you are adding additional CO_2 gas to the grow area. There is more on this in the section previous to this one.

Do not confuse these with carbon monoxide (CO) monitors that are very common household items, often combined with smoke detectors. Carbon dioxide monitors are not as easy to find and will be more expensive, usually starting at around $100 apiece. Small chemical kits are cheaper if you are just periodically checking the air quality. Once you have established a steady and reliable system for adding CO_2, you should not need to have a constant monitor running, but that choice is yours.

Power usage monitors

This is the only item on this list that will not actually have any impact on your growing success. It can have a serious impact on your monthly electric bill though. Lights, pumps, and fans all have a significant power draw to them that leads to one of the main negatives of hydroponic gardening: the cost of electricity. You will not be able to eliminate this issue altogether, but a good voltage meter can go a long way in keeping it under control.

These devices are fairly commonplace and can be purchased at most home renovation or hardware stores. They plug into a wall outlet, and then the device to be tested is plugged into the monitor. After a few moments of operating, the LCD screen will tell you exactly how much power is being drawn. Kill a Watt® is a good brand name, and Blue Planet™ also makes a nice monitor. You would not have one running all the time but you can use it to test the various pieces of equipment periodically to see if anything is drawing more power than you can afford.

You then can lower your overall usage by replacing some items or changing how you run your system.

Fans and Vents

With all these issues involving the air inside your grow space, it should be no surprise that maintain fans and vents will be necessary. Not only do you need to vent out unwanted stale air, you also need to bring in fresh air at the same time. That is, without letting out valuable humidity, heat, or carbon dioxide. It definitely can be more difficult to manage than just cracking a window open.

Not only will you need to move air in and out of the grow room, but you also have to move air around within the room as well. Heat rises and carbon dioxide falls, which will create layers of air through the room that will need to be mixed. Simple room fans are all you need to eliminate this, and those that oscillate work best.

Moving air in and out of the room will be a little more complicated. As mentioned earlier, vents to release hot humid air should be placed higher in the room because heat naturally rises. Add an intake vent lower down to provide a path for better air circulation through the room. All vents should be covered with mesh to keep out insects and other pests. Powered fans can be operated within the vents to keep the air moving if the natural flow of warm and cool air is not enough.

Timers

With so many variables under your control, you will be relying on several different types of timers to keep it all running smoothly. Nobody wants a garden that needs to be attended to every 30 minutes because something needs to be turned on or off. Timers are a vital part of most hydroponics setups.

For something as simple as a daily on/off switch, you can do fine with a standard household timer used to switch lights on and off in a house. The simplest ones have a large dial in the center that turns as time passes. You place small plastic pegs along the rim of the dial so that it triggers the on/off switch as the dial turns. If you have enough pegs, you can have several on and off cycles through the day.

These types of mechanical timers are fine for some lighting applications and some irrigation needs as well, but they will not allow for enough on/off cycles for most types of hydroponics because the water pumps go on and off so frequently and sometimes with time frames too small for the larger timers to manage. If you only need a mister to come on for 30 seconds at a time for example, you will need a more sophisticated timer.

Digital timers are not that much more expensive and can allow for smaller time increments, though most will not handle any time period smaller than one minute.

Another thing to consider with either of these is the voltage requirements of your devices. Inexpensive timers meant for typical household lamps or TVs are not equipped to handle the power that will be required to start up a large wattage fluorescent light bank. You may be able to get away with simple timers for your water pumps, but make sure you invest in good devices to manage your lighting needs. Even so, they are generally not that expensive.

A digital timer from BetterGrow Hydro® can handle most individual lights up to 1200 watts and will only cost around $20. It can be programmed for up to eight cycles a day with time increments as small as one minute. At the other end of the scale would be a $300 repeat cycle timer from Green Air Products. That model allows for much more precise control with cycle duration times of as little as five seconds, and you can run cycles every seven minutes through the day. Optional photo sensors can be added so that the timer only operates during the night or day.

Air Filters

Smaller operations may not need these, but if you are growing a large number of plants, then an air filter can help prevent pollen and other plant debris from accumulating in your growing space. Pollen and smells from the plants can permeate your home, though if your growing room is well-sealed this may not become a problem for you.

A good standard household air filtration unit with a carbon insert should be sufficient for most hobby-sized gardens to keep the air in your grow room clean. It will not only keep odors and dust from traveling to the rest of your house, but it also helps eliminate any spores from the air that might cause a threat to your plants.

If you really want to clean the air, you will want a filter that will also generate ozone or has a UV light for pathogen elimination. Many good units have both. Depending on the model, they are typically installed on your air-intake vent so that all air entering the grow room is cleaned immediately.

These types of air-cleaning units are excessive for a typical indoor hydroponic garden, but if you plan to expand your operation or get into commercial growing, then you should consider getting one.

Water Filters

Your source of water will determine whether you will need to filter your water before using it on your plants. Standard tap water will have chlorine and fluorine added, which is not a healthy additive for your garden. Since using bottled water is not feasible, you should consider having some sort of filter for your water supply. This is not strictly necessary and can be ignored if you do not want the added cost or complexity. You can install a basic one on your tap or under the sink for wherever you intend to get your water (if your grow room does not have its own water supply). Brita® or PUR® units would work well and can be found in most home improvement stores.

You also will need to consider treating your water if your water source has a high amount of dissolved minerals in it (i.e. hard water). Not only will the mineral content interfere with your management of nutrient solution due to the unknown compounds already in the water, but the minerals also will build up a crust on your hoses, fittings, valves, and pots. Technically, this calls for water softening rather than filtration to fix, and water softener systems are fairly common as household appliances. Chapter 3 covers water chemistry, and you can find out more about water hardness there.

YOUR HYDROPONIC GARDEN

I n all likelihood, most hydroponic gardeners will enter in this endeavor with a wish list of the kind of plants they will want to grow in their garden. Some gardeners will want to grow herbs, while others will want to grow flowers. Some gardeners will want to grow a wide variety of plants ranging from fruits and vegetables to herbs and flowers. Chapter 8 will discuss the range of plants best grown in hydroponic gardens and teach you the fundamentals on how to get started growing a variety of plant types. Like any other endeavor as complex as gardening, some activities are easier to manage than others. A good example in this regard is that it is easier to grow lettuce in your hydroponic garden than it is to grow blueberries. Basil is easier to grow than potatoes. It is possible, however, to grow any of these items in your hydroponic garden with a little know-how and experience.

Experience is a vital tool in learning and being successful in your hydroponic gardening endeavor. The old adage, "You must learn to walk before you can run," applies to this practice of hydroponic gardening. As you plan and take your first steps along this path, learn to grow the easy plants first. Yes, there is a difference between growing lettuce and growing carrots in a hydroponic garden, but you will gain vital experience in working with the essential tools and the various components of your garden while enjoying the relatively easy success of growing a delicious variety of lettuce, a plant that is much easier to grow hydroponically than carrots.

Starting Your Plants

You have several options from which to choose when you plan to start planting. You can start your plants from seed, sprouts, or from shoots. Depending on what stage you start at will determine precisely how you start. Some hydroponic gardening systems are better to start your plants at a particular stage, though with some experience, you can start just about anywhere.

You will find that the most rewarding way to start your plants is to start from seeds. You will find that starting your plants from seed will give you a much bigger variety of plants to grow, and it will allow you to gain the experience of the entire cycle of a plant's life. The seed represents the end of a cycle as well as the beginning. Learning how to grow from seed and then to collect

the seeds that the mature plant produces in order to start the cycle anew is also more affordable than buying seeds.

Because you will not be starting seeds in dirt, you will best be served by starting your seeds in starter pots or flats before you place the seedlings in the hydroponic system. You have seen references to seed plugs in the hydroponic systems descriptions in earlier chapters. These plugs are hydroponic planting media with a sprouted plant seedling ready to grow. The reason that you are advised to start your plants in starter pots or flats before placing them in the hydroponic system is that most seeds are very small, and it is easy to lose them or for them to be washed away. Another advantage to starting the seeds in plant pots or in flats is that it allows you to better control the amount of moisture the seed receives.

Because you are engaging in growing your plants hydroponically, or without soil, you should choose to start your seeds in materials that are inorganic. Whether you choose individual starter pots or flats that can accommodate multiple plants, you will fill the given space with the inorganic medium and start the seed in the medium. This seed-planted medium will become the plug that will be placed into your hydroponic gardening system.

It is recommended that you do not use organic matter such as peat or potting soil for your seed plugs, as these materials break down relatively quickly. Materials such as peat and potting soil may be great for soil gardening, but materials that break down can cause problems with any pumps that you may be using in your hydroponic gardening system.

A number of commercial products are available to hydroponic gardeners that are good choices for starter plugs. A few commercially produced starter media include:

- Rapid Root Starter Plugs
- Grodan Rock Wool Starter Cubes
- Perfect Starts
- Oasis Horticubes®

If you review the growing media described in Chapter 5, you will come across several of the media listed above. You also will see in Chapter 5 that there is a selection of media that may work well for more mature plants but will not be suitable for seeds. The medium that is ideal for seeds is a medium that absorbs liquid nutrients well but is not loose. The products listed above are ideal as they are absorbent and are solid pieces of material as opposed to being loose like sand or pebbles.

If you do not choose to go with any of the commercial products listed above, you can choose to purchase sheets of rock wool that can be divided and cut to suit your needs.

Whether you choose to start a single seed or multiple seeds in a tray, you will want to find a dark and warm spot to start your seeds and a well-lighted location to move them to after germination. If you do not have that well-lighted spot, be sure to have a grow light ready to go. Direct sunlight is not advised, but it should be well-lit indirect light. The ideal temperature for your seeds is between 70 and 80 degrees.

The pots or trays you employ will allow for one or two seeds in a small bit of medium. The pots or trays will allow nutrient solution to be absorbed by the medium and also will have holes in the

bottom for drainage. Because the pots or tray will drain, you also should have the pots or trays resting in an irrigation tray.

While you will need to have a well-lit place for your germinated seeds, you also should be able to cover your pots or trays with an opaque lid. Newly planted seeds should be kept in the dark until germination.

If you find that you need to have more control over the temperature of your germinating seeds, you can purchase and employ a heat mat to place beneath the drainage tray. The heat mat can help keep the temperature of the germination pots or trays at a constant ideal temperature.

Another addition to your germination pots and trays you might choose to employ is a humidity dome. Once the seeds have germinated, a clear dome or cover can be used to increase the relative humidity in your new seedling's environment. You can purchase something like a hard clear plastic shell, or you can simply use a piece of plexiglass or glass that fits snuggly over your plants, like a window box. This shell should have small holes in it to allow some amount of airflow.

Once you have all of your component parts, including your chosen seeds, you will take the following steps to get your seeds started:

1. Add your chosen medium (rock wool, Oasis plugs, or whatever medium you have chosen) to the pots or tray cells.
2. Soak the medium in the pots or tray cells with water and allow them to drain before you add your seeds to the medium. Before you add your seeds, see that the medium is wet to the touch but not thoroughly saturated.
3. For most fruits and vegetables, you should place two seeds at the center of each plug located on the pots or tray cells. For herbs, you should place six to eight seeds at the center of each plug. If you are working with very small seeds, you can use a wet toothpick to center the seeds.

4. After the seeds have been placed in the medium, cover the pots or tray with an opaque lid until germination.

5. Keep a close eye on the seed-containing medium, and be sure that it is always damp to the touch. Keep the pots and tray cells moist to the touch.

6. When germination occurs (see chapter 2), you can remove the opaque cover and move the pots or tray to a well-lit place, but not direct sunlight. You also can start using grow lights at this time.

7. After germination occurs, you will start moistening the medium with a mixture of 50 percent water and 50 percent nutrient solution, or a diluted nutrient solution.

8. The seedlings, at this point, also will benefit from a high humidity environment. If you have a clear cover that can be placed over them that will allow light to get in, use it. Again, this cover should have holes that allow airflow.

9. When you start to see leaves form on your plants, remove the seedlings that appear less healthy from each pot or tray cell.

10. You are ready to transplant your plants from germination pots or trays to your hydroponic system once you begin to see roots on the bottoms and sides of the plugs.

Transplanting Your Seedlings into Your Hydroponic System

Transplanting your new plants from the starter pots and/or trays to your chosen hydroponic system is pretty straightforward and simple, but you do have to keep several things in mind when you do this procedure. The plants are fairly hardy and can put up with some amount of mistreatment, but you do need to guard against drying them out and blasting them with light. You also need to take care to place the new seedlings into pots that will be the appropriate size for the plants when they are fully grown.

If you depend on natural sunlight for your plants' growth, do not place them in direct sunlight right away. Light is important, but the heat of direct sunlight will dry the small plants out quickly. Keep in a well-lit place, though not in direct sunlight.

If you will be using grow lights, be sure that the lights are five or six feet above the new plants to start. Every few days you can move the lights a little closer to the plants until they are 18 to 24 inches above your plants.

Choose grow pots that are in keeping with the size of the fully grown plant. Smaller plants, such as herbs might do well in one to five-gallon pots. Plants that will grow larger, such as tomatoes, will demand larger pots that will range from ten to 25 gallons.

To move your seedlings from the starter pots/trays to your chosen hydroponic system, take the following steps:

- Fill the pot(s) that will be used in the hydroponic system with the medium you will be using. You might choose rock wool, expanded clay, perlite, or any one of a combination of growing media as described in Chapter 5.
- Dig a hole in the medium large enough to accommodate the plug that contains the seedling.
- Gently remove the plugs from the starter pot(s)/tray.
- Place the plug directly into the hole you dug in the medium. There is no need to remove the plant from the plug.
- Fill the space around the plug with medium.
- Add water/nutrient solution from above. You can add nutrient solution like you would water a potted plant on a daily basis for about a week until the roots of the plant extend into the nutrients of your hydroponic system. If you are using a top-drip system, you will simply start the drip.

Doing an Internet search for seed companies will get you hundreds, if not thousands, of results. The following is a list of some of the more popular seed purveyors. You will find more information about these companies in the resource section at the back of this book.

- Burpee®
- De Ruiter™ Seeds
- High Mowing Organic Seeds
- Johnny's Selected Seeds
- Ornamental Edibles

- Richters
- Rijk Zwaan
- Stokes® Seeds

Using Store-Bought Seedlings in Your Hydroponic Gardening System

There are many advantages to starting your plants from seed in the manner described above:

- Starting from seed is more cost effective than buying seedlings from a garden store, especially if you start from seeds that have been saved from plants that you grew. (Saving seeds will be discussed in Chapter 9.)
- You will find that you have will have a greater selection of plants and varieties of plants from which to choose if you decide to start from seed. Your options for seedling purchase will be somewhat limited.
- When you purchase seedlings, you cannot be sure that you are purchasing a healthy plant that is free of pest infestation. It is easier to protect against these threats if you start from seed. If you bring diseased and/or pest infested plants into your home or greenhouse, there is great danger that they will spread to other plants. Some diseases and pests are very difficult to eliminate.
- Plants that you start from seed will be in the type of medium that you choose. Plants that you purchase as seedlings will, more than likely, be in an organic medium such as peat or soil that you will need to remove from the plant roots before you place them in your hydroponic system. Often, young plants have a difficult time

withstanding this rough transplant. Melons, squash, herbs, lettuce, and legumes will all have a difficult time after having their roots disturbed in this manner.

If you do choose to purchase seedlings from a store, you should take the following precautions:

- Purchase an insecticidal soap and a houseplant and garden spray to rid your plants of any insects that may be present.
- Apply the sprays to your plants inside, but not in your grow room. DO NOT BRING THE PLANTS INTO THE GROW ROOM UNTIL YOU HAVE TREATED THEM BY SATURATING THEM TO ERADICATE THE PEST THREAT.
- When you are ready to transplant your seedlings, carefully break off the peat pots they have been started in. Do this to each plant one at a time so that the roots of the young plant will not have time to dry out before you get it safely into its new grow pot.
- Be very careful as you remove as much soil as possible from the newly formed root system. As you remove the soil, you can do so under a gentle wash of room temperature to warm water.
- After you have removed most of the soil, place the seedling into the medium you already have prepared in your hydroponic system. Gently fill the medium in around the roots of the newly replanted seedling.

What to Grow?

The answer to this question of "what to grow?" is, of course, "Anything I want to!" There are, however, plants that are easier to grow in hydroponic systems and plants that are recommended for the hydroponic novice.

Plants recommended for those new to hydroponic gardening are plants that can be grown in a wide variety of hydroponic system types, are easy to start by seed, are easy to maintain, have a relatively quick grow time, take little space, and are forgiving of grower errors. This might seem to a pretty hefty list of requirements for the novice looking for an easy way into learning more about hydroponic gardening, but the list of plants that fit these requirements is quite lengthy.

Generally, the beginning hydroponic gardener can start by growing herbs, lettuces, and/or small ornamental plants. The list of specific plants might include:

- Parsley
- Basil
- Dill
- Cilantro
- Bibb lettuce

- Iceberg lettuce
- Romaine
- African violets
- Begonias
- Zinnias
- Bamboo

This is, of course, a very short list that could be much longer. The plants mentioned above are just a small example of the herbs, lettuce varieties, and ornamental plants that you might consider starting as a novice hydroponic grower.

As you gain a firmer understanding of how hydroponics works and how different systems work for you and your plants, you can consider growing your operations to include a larger variety of fruits, vegetables, herbs, and ornamental plants.

You will find that most plants that you would normally grow outdoors in a garden can be grown successfully hydroponically. Even so, here is a list of most common plants that will thrive in a water-based gardening system:

Artichokes	Cauliflower
Asparagus	Celery
Beans, green	Cucumber
Beans, dry	Eggplant
Beets	Endive
Blueberries	Garlic
Broccoli	Kale
Brussels sprouts	Leeks
Cabbage	Lettuce
Carrots	Okra

Onion

Parsnip

Peas

Peppers, sweet

Peppers, hot

Potatoes

Radishes

Raspberries

Spinach

Squashes

Strawberries

Sweet potatoes

Tomatoes

Fruit trees can be started with hydroponics to create strong seedlings, but standard size trees will need outdoor planting. Small dwarf trees may be able to grow to a harvestable age within a hydroponics system as long as you address their size and keep them pruned. Herbs of any type, as well as most flowering plants, can be grown without much restriction.

Certain vegetables such as corn, zucchini, pumpkins, and most melons are not that practical because they take up too much space. That is not to say they cannot be grown. If you have the room and can be a little creative with plant supports, you may be successful even with these plants. Once you learn more about hydroponics, you could try taking them on as a personal challenge.

As a novice reading about the potential cornucopia of harvests to come, you either will feel overwhelmed by the possibilities of what to grow, or you will be inspired to dive in and plant as wide a variety of plants as you have the space to accommodate. However you choose to proceed, a good rule of green thumb is to begin by planting things your family appreciates. If you enjoy cooking, start by preparing a small hydroponic system in your kitchen (if there is space and the proper amount of light) and planting a small herb garden. Growing items such as chives, parsley, oregano, and basil right in your kitchen will allow you to snip and use them in your recipes for the freshest, best-tasting herbs to be added to your family meals.

Another upside of starting a small hydroponic herb garden in your kitchen is that kitchens are frequently the busiest room of the house. It is easy to keep a close eye on the progress (or lack of progress) of your plants. Also, it gets everyone in the household interested in the growth of the plants.

Once you get the hang of hydroponics through your kitchen herb garden and you become accustomed to tending to your plants, you can consider expanding your hydroponic operations to other plants in other areas of your house, porch, patio, and/or yard. If you do expand your garden to include both indoor and outdoor plants, be very careful about how you handle the plants you grow outside relative to pests. You do not want to introduce the  pests that will enjoy your outdoor plants to the relatively clean indoor plants. Be sure to wash any harvested plants outdoors before you bring them indoors.

Greenhouses

If you become adept at growing and enthusiastic about expanding your hydroponic operations, there may come a time when you will wish to employ a greenhouse. Greenhouses can come in many different shapes and styles. Like growing in any other media that have been described in this chapter, you can choose to construct your own greenhouse or purchase one from a retailer.

If you choose to construct a greenhouse, make sure you enclose your garden completely in a clear bubble. A simple plastic wrapping can work for this, but it is better to construct a larger area that will provide more circulation. This is easily accomplished with several coat hangers and heavy-duty plastic wrap. Your goal is simply to surround your hydroponic system in a clear bubble; it is not necessary that the tent is airtight.

If you choose to purchase a greenhouse that you can use in your home or apartment, you can buy one starting at about $40. *See the Appendix for information on where to find this product.*

Making an Indoor Greenhouse

There are simple instructions that describe a way of putting together a basic indoor greenhouse for a single plant, but with a little imagination and very little cost, you can make an indoor greenhouse that will allow you to accommodate numerous plants.

There is always the option of purchasing an indoor greenhouse and greenhouse supplies. If you would like to consider this option, check out the mini-greenhouses at **www.hydro farm.com**.

If you are handy and would rather build it yourself, you can do it with things that you already have around the house or that are easily available at your local hardware store or supermarket.

You simply need to provide a frame of some sort and a way to enclose the frame in such a way that sunlight gets in. For a frame, you might consider an open shelving unit (such as utility shelves) or a table (such as a card table) turned upside down. You can enclose the frame with a clear plastic shower curtain or two. The plastic covering can be secured with tacks, clothespins, or any other device that allows for easy manipulation.

When you enclose the frame, be sure that you arrange an easy access to your greenhouse as you will need to water and care for your plants. Access means that you also can open the enclosed space to regulate, to some degree, the temperature. (To monitor the temperature, place a thermometer in the middle of the greenhouse in a place that is easily visible.) Place the greenhouse in a location in your home or apartment that allows for maximum sunlight.

A number of greenhouse plans available online describe more elaborate setups with grow lights and heaters. These more elaborate greenhouses are a little more difficult to build but give you greater ability to control the greenhouse environment.

When it comes to planning your greenhouse/hydroponic system combination, choose a method and experiment with it. Try another, and see how you like it. You will find that no matter which method you choose or what equipment you decide upon, hydroponic gardening is easy and relatively inexpensive. Before you run out and purchase an expensive hydroponic system, see how easy it is to make your own. Like most people who grow hydroponic gardens, you probably will find that growing plants in a soil-free environment is easy and economical.

A Soil-Free Growing Experiment

If you are completely new to the practice of hydroponic gardening and would like to engage in a little experiment to see if it is something that you would enjoy, you can do this simple and rewarding experiment in your kitchen. This experiment combines many of the basic principles described in this book so far: sprouting, simple hydroponic growing, and greenhouse growing. These are all accomplished over a relatively short period for very little expense.

You can grow any of the crops listed earlier in this chapter without soil. Grasses and sunflower greens can be grown hydroponically in a simple greenhouse in much the same manner as the chinampas of the central Mexican plains that were described in chapter 1. "Chinampas," you will recall, is combined chinamitl (reed basket) and pan (upon). These reed baskets made floating gardens and were early forms of hydroponic gardening systems.

If you are interested in experimenting, you can perform this experiment using a soil-based basket and one soil-free to see what the taste difference is of the plants that you grow from the same seed stock. You may find this an interesting experiment because you will discover what soil does for the taste of these items. Some people will swear by the soil-free method of growing and the resulting taste, while others will swear that soil-free growing tastes like cardboard, and soil makes all the difference. However, the difference in taste is very difficult to account for, so you will need to be the judge. Follow these simple instructions to grow wheat-grass and sunflower greens soil-free, and compare them to what you grow in soil.

Necessities

- Jar
- Basket (This basket needs to be a large bamboo basket with a wide weave. The bamboo should be natural, with no paint or coating of any kind)
- Greenhouse tent (The requirement here is that you enclose your garden completely in a clear bubble. Simple plastic wrap can work for this, but it is better to construct a larger area that will provide more circulation. This is easily accomplished with several coat hangers and heavy-duty plastic wrap. Your goal is simply to surround your basket of sprouts in a clear bubble; it is not necessary that the tent be airtight)
- Measuring cup

- Sieve
- ½ cup of organic sunflower seeds, oat, rye, or wheat
- Colander
- Water (If you live in a place with clean and reliable drinking tap water, using it is perfectly fine. If you should not drink your tap water, use bottled drinking water)

Procedure

1. Examine sunflower seeds or grains to be sprouted, discarding any discolored seeds, hulls, broken seeds, or any foreign matter.
2. Place the sunflower seeds or grains in a bowl, and cover with water.
3. Allow the sunflower seeds to sit in the water for ten minutes.
4. Pour the sunflower seeds and water from the bowl into a sieve and run cool water over the seeds to clean them.
5. Place sunflower seeds in wide-mouth jar.
6. Cover the top of the jar with a plastic strainer top. (You also can use cheesecloth or any top that will allow the sprouting grain to breathe and be used as a strainer.)
7. Add two to three cups of cool water to jar.
8. Soak the sunflower seeds or grains for eight to 12 hours.
9. Pour the water off through the strainer top, leaving the sunflower seeds in the jar. As you pour the water off, swirl the sunflower seeds around in the jar.
10. Rinse and drain the sprouts.
11. Fill the jar of sunflower seeds or grains with water.

12. Pour the soaked sunflower seed or grains and water into the basket to drain.

13. Tip the basket one way and then the other as the water drains for several minutes.

14. Place the basket into a completely enclosed clear tent.

15. The greenhouse can be set in an out-of-the-way location at room temperature for two or three days. The location of the greenhouse should be shaded, though it is not necessary to keep it in the dark.

16. Keep your greenhouse watered during this period by giving your little sprouts good showers. The sprouts require more than a misting; they need a good rain. Do not use the hard run of a faucet, but employ a scattered shower. The goal here is to give them a good rinsing. (The only time your sprouts should be out of their greenhouse is when they are being watered.)

17. The greenhouse should remain in a shaded area for about four days.

18. After four days, place the greenhouse in a well-lit place in indirect sunlight for four or five days.

19. Water the greens daily during this period. Again, they require a hearty shower.

20. After the eighth day (four days of shade and four days of sun), you will notice that your sprouts have rooted themselves in the basket. If you turn the basket upside down and brush it gently, the hulls will fall. You can even dip your basket in cool water to give the sprouts a bath.

21. By the ninth day, you can harvest your garden.

22. To harvest the greens, grab bunches of sprouts and gently wiggle them free of the basket. You will leave

roots behind that can be cleaned out of the basket by cutting with a pair of scissors.

23. Place the sprouts in a bowl of cool water to rinse. Move them around with your fingers to release the remaining hulls.

24. Drain the sprouts in a colander.

25. Allow the sprouts to dry for at least eight hours before you refrigerate them.

26. Store the produce in a glass container in the refrigerator for up to two weeks, though it is best consumed as soon as possible.

Growing Your Hydroponic Gardening System

Once you have determined that hydroponic gardening is for you, the sky is the limit. The small experiment you engaged in as described above; your small kitchen hydroponic herb garden; your small patio hydroponic greenhouse have all gained you experience and gotten you into the hydroponic habit of starting, monitoring, tending, and harvesting your hydroponically grown plants. The experience gained through these simple first steps will lead you not only to the satisfaction derived from learning a new skill and growing your own food, but it also will pave the path from "novice" to "expert."

CASE STUDY: JOSE GERARD

Jose Gerard
Growzay's Aquaponics
www.growzaysaquaponics.com

My hydroponic grow operation is known as Aquaponics. Aquaponics is a hydroponic system that relies on fish as the nutrient suppliers. I grow veggies all year round. My system is set up outside. It is currently in its 3rd year of production.

I use a media based and (NFT) nutrient film technique system hybrid. It is a one of a kind design. It is two systems in one combined to ensure the healthiest of crops. The Growzay Hydroponic/Aquaponic System has many advantages over the other types of hydroponic systems.

The main difference and advantage is that one does not need to use expensive fertilizers in order to grow plants and veggies. The fish supply the nutrients by living in the reservoir and their effluent or fish waste is pumped up to the grow beds along with super oxygenated water. Then the hydroton (grow rocks) that the plants grow in serve as a bio filter, allowing many surfaces for the much-needed beneficial bacteria to colonize. They break down/convert the ammonia into nitrites and then into nitrates that is a readily usable plant food — nitrogen. The roots in the rocks clean and purify the water before it is drained back into the reservoir for the fish to be recycled again over and over, which is controlled by a timer.

There are no disadvantages to hydroponic gardening that I know of with my system.

I became interested in hydroponic gardening back in 1990. That is when I set out to invent my own unique system. Hydroponics allows anyone to grow a garden with little to no experience. My system makes it very easy for anyone to master hydroponic/aquaponic growing.

The Growzay's Hydroponic & Aquaponic System utilizes a top feed nutrient delivery system (via submersible pump), which is gravity drained into a reservoir. The growbed is comprised of individual growing trays which makes it very easy and accessible for crop rotation for perpetual harvests, This system not only has plenty of room in each of its individual modular grow trays for initial explosive root growth in the early stages of plant life, but the (secret) also is that the roots grow in the hydroton-filled trays and form a thick mat of roots providing the plants stability and a great found

The most common mistake for beginners at hydroponic growing is that they add too much pH up or down, and they end up doing damage to the chemistry of the water, which affects the plants' growth. With Aquaponics, the managing of the water quality is much easier and forgiving.

Aquaponics is becoming the obvious choice of urban gardeners who are serious about family food production. It is now gaining worldwide recognition as being the most practical path toward being food self-reliant. With the recent droughts and food prices on the rise, it just makes common sense to implement this unique opportunity to help you with your family needs.

Growzay's Aquaponic System will enable you to achieve success. It's reliable, easy to set up and maintain, and yes, organic. Think green. Go green. Be green!

PLANT PROPAGATION

ow that you have successfully grown several crops in a variety of ways, you can start to think about the many avenues open to you with regard to sustainability. Just like with traditional gardening, you have a few options to propagate your plants to keep your indoor garden going. Plant propagation saves the gardener from having to buy seeds for every growing season. Another topic that will be discussed in Chapter 9 is the difference between growing perennials and annuals in a hydroponic garden.

The cycle of life, in terms of your garden, starts with a seed. The seed sprouts and grows into a plant. The plant grows and produces seeds that ensure the continuation of the plant's line. If, as a gardener, you find that the plant produces a tasty tomato, a vibrant flower, or a particularly hot cayenne pepper, it only makes sense that you would want to continue the line of that plant. Simply going out and buying more seeds from the same vendor and the same seed company does not ensure that you will get the same results. To ensure that you get that same heat from your hydroponically grown cayenne pepper, you can save the seeds of several peppers produced by your healthy plants. Another way to continue the line of the plants you enjoy is to clone them by taking and replanting cuttings. However you choose to proceed in propagating the plants you enjoy, these methods are simple and rewarding.

Saving Seeds

There are many answers to the question: Why should one save seeds? After all, seeds are relatively inexpensive. It is easier, perhaps, to just pick up a few packets at your local hardware or gardening store. Also, it seems that we always have the need to plant something new.

On the other hand, when you buy seeds from the hardware store, you do not know exactly what you are getting. If you buy a package of tomato seeds, you know you are getting tomatoes, but you cannot be sure about the quality of the tomato. You do not know the flavor, the texture, the heartiness of the plant. When you use seeds you have saved from a plant you have been happy with, you can be assured that the likelihood of the plant behaving in much the same way as its forbearer is fairly certain. While it is true that many variables are at play when it comes to a plant's genetics, you will be able to control many of those variables, as you will be growing your plants in the relatively stable environment of your hydroponic garden.

If you were going to plant your seeds in your backyard garden, a great many more variables would come into play, such as the

bees that carry pollen from the tomatoes in your neighbor's yard and the birds that drop competing seeds in your garden. In your controlled hydroponic environment, however, you are the master.

As for the need to plant something new, this is common and understood. That said, saving seeds is a little like returning to that favorite recipe time and time again. If you have a favorite recipe for Hungarian goulash that you and your family love and derive comfort from, why look for a different recipe for Hungarian goulash? Disappointment almost certainly will follow as you compare it to your favorite recipe.

When it comes to seed saving, there are two very easy procedures to follow. The type of plant you are working with will determine which procedure. Much of the information offered here comes from the The Seed Ambassadors Project.

The Seed Ambassadors Project is a group of individuals who have recognized that saving seeds is the foundation of developing durable and resilient locally based food systems. They encourage others to join them in this important work. In their eyes, every seed saved is a socially healing, community-creating event. See their website at **www.seedambassadors.org** for an extensive rundown of the project.

The Seed Ambassadors Project members are not trained botanists, but they have learned from their own experiments and experiences as well as from some of the best seed savers and plant breeders in the world.

Based near Crawfordsville, Oregon, The Seed Ambassadors Project comprises organic farmers and gardeners, simultaneously acting as the seed stewards of more 1,000 varieties of food crops. You can check out their commercial seed list at **www.adaptive seeds.com**.

Some of the information offered here is more relevant to soil-based growing, but all the information is instructive for harvesting and saving seed for use in your hydroponic garden. Also, much of the information here is instructive in regard to plant genetics and garden maintenance.

What Seeds to Save

As you begin to explore the question of "What seeds should I save?" you will, no doubt, come across the big issue of genetics. Genetics is a branch of the science of biology and concerns variations among living organisms determined by genes and heredity. Delve too far into the study of genetics as you try to determine which seeds to save and you may become hopelessly mired in a complex maze that will confuse you to the point of desperation. Leave genetics to the biologists.

The primary rule when it comes to saving seeds is that healthy seeds come from healthy plants. Do not save seeds from plants that are weak or show signs of any disease. Plants that are healthy, vigorous, and have produced healthy fruit will produce the most viable seeds.

When you start to think about saving seeds from a particular crop, ask yourself:

- Did the current crop produce plants, fruit, and seeds in a relatively successful manner?
- Did a high percentage of the seeds germinate and grow to maturity?
- Did the plants grow from vigorous seedlings?
- Were the seeds that the plants produced fully formed and large relative to the plant type?
- Did the seeds get everything they needed as the plant matured?

It is vital to consider the germination rate of the current crop as you think about saving seeds for your next planting. If the previous batch of seeds were viable enough to have a high germination rate, there is a greater likelihood that the seeds you collect from them will also show the same viability.

Likewise, once those seeds have germinated, determine how vigorously they grew to seedlings. If the plants went from germinated seeds to seedlings in a vigorous manner, you can be fairly certain that the next generation of plants will behave in a similar manner.

Viability, vitality, and a vigorous nature are all passed from generation to generation. These are inherited genetic traits. As a gardener, a hydroponic gardener, you do have some influence over the passing of these traits from generation to generation. You are responsible for providing the best environment possible to ensure a plant's health and well-being. You are also responsible for allowing the plant to mature fully before you collect seeds.

To ensure that the seeds you plant are as viable as possible, germinate, and become vigorous seedlings, it is vital that you allow the seeds to be fully formed before you collect them. Do not remove the seeds from the parent plant until the seeds are ready. As a plant begins to produce seeds, it is drawing energy from its environment and channeling that energy into the seed. The nutrients you are feeding the plant and the energy it is drawing from the light is going directly into the seed. The longer that seed can remain with its parent plant, the greater its viability and the more vigor it will have as it becomes its own seedling and starts the cycle all over again.

Why Save Seeds?

We are losing diversity, biological and social, at an unprecedented rate. This erosion of diversity directly limits our ecological and social resilience and adaptability within this changing world.

According to the United Nations Food and Agricultural Organization, crop genetic resources are disappearing at the rate of one to two percent a year. About 75 percent of agricultural crop diversity is estimated to have been lost since the beginning of the last century. Saving seeds is a powerful way to counteract this problem and has a profound effect on our future resilience and sustainability. We need genetic diversity in our gardens, farms, and kitchens in order to recreate resilient healthy food systems and people.

Saving seeds is easy. Whether you are an experienced farmer or a new gardener with a handful of plants, you can save seeds.

The "easy seed" types in the list that follows all are truly easy. The "less easy seed" is still easy if you follow a few simple techniques. After all, seed saving is one of the most fundamental human (and squirrel) activities, practiced long before the idea of formal schooling was invented. Even many

ancient non-agrarian cultures still saved seeds to some extent to manage wild plant populations.

Some fruits, such as tomatoes and melons, have mature seeds inside them. These only require minimal processing before you can store or sow them. Other plants, like snap peas and green beans, usually are eaten before the seeds have matured inside them. You simply can forget to harvest a few pods, let them dry on the plant, and a few weeks later, collect the seeds. Other seeds are a bit more complicated than that.

The hope is that this seed-saving guide will provide you with the knowledge and inspiration to save seed from myriad common and not so common edible food crops. After you learn many of the common crops, uncommon crops become intuitive.

From our experience, enthusiasm may cause one to become overwhelmed with the opportunity to save seed from EVERYTHING. This is perfectly normal. We suggest taking a step back and starting with one or two types of plants from the "easy seed" section. Really getting to know a crop is a valuable thing to do and yields endless entertainment. Or just jump in and try it all. Do not get discouraged if things do not workout all the time, old wisdom can be hard to rekindle. Also, plants dying is often a good thing when it comes to stewarding a seed. It is a selection event, selecting the hardy ones for next generation.

You soon will discover that the rewards of saving seeds are far greater than the efforts extended, from money saved by not purchasing seed to the joy of experiencing a plant living through its entire life cycle, stewarded along by your helping hand.

"Food Sovereignty is Seed Sovereignty."

How to Steward a Seed

For plants that usually are eaten in the vegetative stage, all you have to do is eat the seconds and let the best plants make seed. For plants that we eat the fruit of, such as tomatoes and melons, eat and save seed from the best-tasting fruits. Expose your plants to selection pressures (natural and human caused) and see how the plants adapt to your growing conditions. If you save seed from the best-flavored and healthiest plants you will be stacking the deck in your favor for next season and, for future generations of plants and people.

Why Steward Seed?

You fully choose what you grow and the characteristics of what you grow, thereby escaping dependency on seed companies. You may not believe it at first, but your garden is much more dependable than a seed company. Often, one grower and distributor produces all of the seed for one variety for the entire U.S. seed market. If there is a crop failure on that mega seed farm then the favorite bean you have been growing for years may be gone for good. Varieties often degenerate in the hands of big producers. They do not have time to select them for good flavor or other characteristics you love in a particular variety. The classic example is the delicata squash seed that was grown a few years back. It was contaminated with extremely bitter genetics. There was only one grower in the country that year, and the line was completely ruined. The industry had to go back to seed savers to repair the line. This kind of thing happens all the time.

Fundamental Seed Saving Concepts

You need to know a few fundamentals when saving seeds. Once you are familiar with these concepts, you can easily and successfully save just about any seeds you want.

Peruse the glossary section for more concept explanations.

Open pollinated (OP), heirloom, and hybrid (F1)

Open-pollinated (OP) plants are plants that are allowed to reproduce according to the whims of the bees and the wind, or whatever pollination mechanism they depend on. Open-pollinated can refer to self-pollinating plants (tomatoes and beans), or crosspollinating plants (cabbages and beets). OP usually is used to describe plants that are not hybrids. OP seeds can be just as vigorous, disease resistant, and commercially useful as hybrids if properly stewarded.

Heirloom refers to a variety of plant (or animal) that has been passed down from generation to generation. Usually a minimum of three (human) generations is required for a plant to be known as an heirloom, but the term also may refer to old (more than 100 years) commercial varieties. All heirlooms are OP, but not all OP varieties are heirlooms.

Hybrid (or F1) refers to plant (or animal) varieties that are achieved by crossing two distinct inbred lines. This results in increased uniformity and sometimes vigor and disease resistance. Seed saved from hybrids will not grow true-to-type. Hybrids are used extensively in industrial farming because they are uniform and yield all at the same time, which is good for grocery stores. Hybrids are also good for seed companies because they create proprietary control over the seed. If a farmer wants to grow a hybrid variety she or he must purchase new seed from that company every year. Hybrid seed is usually more expensive and is often bred for shipping and shelf life, not flavor or nutrition.

Crossers and selfers

Some plants are out-breeding/cross-pollinating, which is to say the flowers they produce usually do not fertilize themselves. They depend upon having a large population and, in the case of insect-pollinated plants, the participation of sufficient pollinators to get the job done. Crossers may be insect-pollinated, wind-pollinated, or both. They may have perfect flowers (containing both male and female parts, as in the case of carrots or broccoli) or imperfect flowers (male and female parts found in different places, as is the case with corn or spinach, which has male and female plants). Only one variety per species of a crosser should flower at a time if seed purity is one of your objectives.

Selfers, or self-pollinating plants, always have perfect flowers. The flowers usually pollinate themselves before they open, but sometimes depend on pollinators to trigger pollination. Some selfers can be cross-pollinated depending on conditions, such as temperature or the friskiness of pollinators present. Bumblebees have been known to tear bean flowers open and cross-pollinate flowers before self-pollination has occurred. When saving seed, many varieties of a self-pollinating species usually can be grown at the same time.

Dry and wet and fermentation seed processing

To save seed there are only three simple processes to know. Once you have an understanding of each of the processes, you can save almost any seed.

1. Dry seed processing refers to seed that dries down on the plant and needs to be kept dry until it is sown. The steps involved are harvesting (usually cutting the seed stalk off of the plant), threshing (separating the seed from the stalk and chaff), and winnowing (removing the seed from the chaff using a breeze). Dry seed processing is used for grains, lettuce, brassicas, onions, beets, carrots, celery, cilantro, and chicories, among others.

2. Wet seed processing is the process by which the seeds of many garden fruits are saved. This includes melons, peppers, eggplant, tomatillo, and squash seed. Wet seed processing involves removing the seed from the fruit, rinsing it clean of debris, and then drying. A jar of water can be used to separate seed from debris — seeds sink, and debris usually floats. Drying the seed quickly and completely after wet processing is very important.

3. Fermentation seed processing is similar to wet seed processing, but the seeds and their juices (as in tomato and sometimes melons and cucumbers) are mixed with a little water and allowed to ferment for a day or two. The fermentation process breaks down germination inhibitors such as the gel-sack that surrounds tomato seeds. When a layer of mold has formed on top of the water and the seeds sink, the fermentation is complete. You simply need to add more water, swish it around, then decant the mold and pulp. You may need to repeat this process several times, as the good seeds sink to the bottom and the scum floats off the top. After all

the pulp, bad seeds, and mold is removed, drain the water from the seeds, and set them out on a plate, screen, or paper towel to dry. Once the seeds are thoroughly dry, place them in a moisture-proof container, label, and store them for the future.

Annuals and biennials and perennials

Annuals are plants that complete their life cycle (produce seed and die) in one growing season. Many of the garden fruits and vegetables we eat are annuals, such as lettuce, beans, peas, squashes, cucumbers, melons, basil, cilantro, summer broccoli, potatoes, and annual radishes. In cooler climates, tomatoes and peppers are annuals.

Biennials are plants that require two seasons to complete their life cycle (produce seed and die). This includes: cabbages, onions, leeks, beets, parsnips, celery, parsley, rutabagas, and carrots. Biennials are usually insect- or wind-pollinated and require dry processing.

Perennials are plants that live for a minimum of three years, but some can live for decades. They usually can produce seed and not die. Common edible perennials include many herbs, such as oregano and rosemary; tree fruits like apples and pears; berries, rhubarb, artichoke, and asparagus; as well as tomatoes and peppers in warm climates. The term perennial includes herbaceous ornamental plants we usually call "perennials," as well as trees, bulbs, shrubs, cacti, bamboos, some grasses, and vines.

The pedigree and the adaptivar

When saving seed, it is important to be clear about what you are trying to achieve. Do you want to maintain varietal integrity and keep a variety pure? This is necessary if you want to preserve a rare variety. In this case, you need to make sure to have proper isolation distances between outbreeders and have sufficient population size.

If maintaining a pedigree line is not your goal, it may be wise to steward an adaptivar. An adaptivar is a collection of several varieties of a cross-pollinating species that are allowed to cross-pollinate with each other, thereby producing plants with a large degree of genetic variation. The genetic variation is so diverse that you are getting new crosses with each generation. Though the plants produced from adaptivars are not uniform or stable and likely will not breed true-to-type, they are useful because they are vigorous and will have enough variation that some of them may be able to thrive in less than ideal circumstances.

Pedigrees, on the other hand, tend to be less resilient over time in adverse growing conditions. Ancient adaptivars, sometimes referred to as landraces, are where most of our agricultural genetic diversity originated. This is often the chosen stewardship mode of indigenous cultures and subsistence farmers. True seed stewardship embraces the selection events nature presents as the means to reconnect to the evolutionary relationships between the ecology and its organisms. Another benefit to adaptivars is that they offer a variety of flavor. And you always can select down from the pool to develop a distinct pedigree.

A little bit about storage

Storage is possibly the most critical aspect of seed saving. Yet it is as simple as dry, cool, pest-free, and labeled.

Dry, very dry

Small seeds can be left out for a few dry days and sealed into their bag or jar once they feel crispy dry. Old window screens, cookie sheets, or plates all work well for this. Larger seeds need more help. Use a dehydrator or fan. Be careful, because heat above 100 degrees F can damage seed viability. Direct sunlight by itself has not been shown to harm seed viability, but it is better to avoid it because temperature swings in full sun can cook naked seeds.

Airflow is the most important consideration when drying seeds. The ideal seed-drying conditions would be cool DRY air flowing through and around the seeds.

Cool, cold, or frozen

Genebanks keep their seeds in sub-zero freezers, and this can keep a seed viable for 50 or more years. Although deep freezers are not necessary, keep your seeds as cool as possible. The coolest room in the house, basement, or the garage is sometimes the best option. Have extra room in the freezer? Dry your seeds down completely and stick them in. Warning: damp seeds will die if frozen.

Kill seed-eating bugs

The easiest way to keep insects from eating your seeds is to get them dry and then freeze them for three days. This is most important with large seeds like corn, beans, and peas. Be careful not to open the cold seed container until it warms up to room temperature. Some people have had success with CO_2 when dealing with large quantities. All you need is a home-brewing friend to borrow a CO_2 tank from. With the seed in a bucket, add a fair amount of CO_2 by pressing the valve in the bucket for five seconds. Put a lid on it to prevent air from mixing back into it. CO_2 is heavier than air and sinks, forcing out the air. After a few days, it will have killed any bugs.

Choose a good container and label well

Reused glass jars work great. Ziploc® bags put in small hard plastic totes, also work well. This keeps mice away and is space efficient. Labeling is very important when you save more than a few varieties. Masking tape and Sharpies® are indispensible. Putting crispy dry pieces of paper as labels inside the bags acts as a light desiccant. If you pull them out and they are not crispy dry, then your seeds are a still bit damp.

Useful Tools for Seed Saving

- Buckets or totes — for collecting into and for winnowing
- Jars or small plastic tubs/yogurt containers — for fermenting and wet processing seed .
- Plate or baking sheet or window screen — for seed drying
- Airtight containers and/or envelopes — for storing seeds
- Tarps — drying seed heads, catching seed, or winnowing onto
- Hardware cloth screen — for screening seeds from debris
- Masking Tape — for labeling
- Sturdy storage container — protection from mice
- Sieve or fine mesh strainer — to drain water from wet seeds
- Box fan — for when there is no consistent wind for winnowing

- Food dehydrator — for drying seeds to ideal (low) moisture content for storage. Must set thermostat lower than 95 degrees
- Pruners — important for clipping, picking, cutting, and harvesting

Seed Specifics

Tomatoes Lycopersicon esculentum

Saving tomato seed is easy. An in-season, ripe, organic tomato is often a consumer's first introduction to real organic food. Success growing a tomato is often a new gardener's introduction into heavier gardening. Saving seed of a favorite tomato variety is often a new seed saver's introduction into heavier seed saving. To top it off, ripe tomatoes from the garden and farmer's market come complete with mature seeds inside. Be aware, though, that most commercially available tomatoes are hybrids, and the seed you save from these fruits will not produce fruit identical to the one you saved seed from. Also, most tomatoes from the grocery store are bred to hold their shape and color through the rigors of mechanical harvesting, transport, and distribution, and usually taste quite bland. Be sure to taste the tomato before you save the seeds.

Heirloom and open-pollinated tomatoes are, by definition, not hybrids and usually taste delicious, so save seed voraciously. To save tomato seed:

1. Cut the fruit in half.
2. Use your finger or a knife to scoop out the seeds and juice from their cavities, or squeeze the tomato over a

glass jar. Use a small jar, such as a jelly jar, if you are only saving seeds from one or two tomatoes.

3. Once the seeds and all their juicy juice is in the jar, add no more than 25 percent water, and slosh it around.

4. Place the jar someplace warm for two or three days.

5. Every day, check on the concoction, and stir it a little.

6. After a few days (depending on the weather), a mold should form on the top. This method mimics the rotting of the tomato in nature or the actions of the digestive system of an animal and breaks down the clear gel coat around the seeds, which prevents the seed from sprouting inside the tomato or in your stomach.

7. Once the mold covers the entire top of the liquid and the seeds have begun to sink, the gel coat has been broken down, and they are ready for cleaning. Be careful not to leave the seeds in the jar too long at this point because once the gel coat is broken down the seeds may sprout in the jar, and you will have to start over.

8. You know seeds are ready for their final cleaning when most of them have sunk to the bottom of the jar.

9. Add water to fill the jar, and slosh it around.

10. Let it settle for a moment.

11. Carefully pour the water out of the jar. The mold, pulp, and immature seeds all will flow out with the water, but the mature seeds should sink and stay in the jar.

12. Repeat this decanting process two to five times until you have only clean seeds and clean water.

13. Pour out as much water as you can without losing the seeds, or pour it through a fine mesh strainer.

14. Pat the seeds dry through the strainer, and then scoop the seeds out on a small plate.

15. Allow the seeds to dry without intense heat.
16. When the seeds are very dry, store the seeds in a moisture-proof container in a cool, dry place.
17. It is very important to label the container with variety and date. Tomato seeds can last for ten years or more if stored cool and dry.

Another easy way to save tomato seed is to spit out a few seeds on a square of tissue as you are eating the tomato. Just let the seeds dry down on their own, and they will stick to the tissue. This method is convenient because you can write the date and type of tomato right on the tissue. BUT, because you have skipped the fermentation process, you will get lower germination, so make sure to save and sow extra if you use this process. You also will get sticky seeds stuck to paper, which is kind of problematic, but you can plant the piece of tissue when it is sowing time.

Beans and peas

Common beans and peas are among the easiest plants to save seed from. If you have peas and beans in your hydroponic garden, all you have to do is forget to pick some toward the end of the growing cycle and let them dry down on the plant. For better quality and a higher seed yield, set aside a few of the best whole plants for seed saving. When you pull up the plant at the end of the growing cycle, dried seeds will be ready for you to save. All you have to do is shell them from the pod. Make sure the pods are crispy dry, or the seed may not be as mature as would be ideal.

Snap peas and beans picked for market for fresh eating do not have mature seed, so you cannot simply dry these down and plant them. You can plant any dry beans you grow or buy from the grocery store, such as pinto beans or black beans. Dried peas from the grocer also can be planted, but make sure they are not split peas.

No hybrid beans or peas are available for sale, so you are sure to get the same variety as you planted. Unless of course, there was a frisky bumblebee around,

For the best storage of peas and beans, the seeds must be very dry. They must shatter when hit by a hammer and not squish. Then dry freeze them for ten days to kill bean weevils that may be living inside the seed. Seal in a moisture-proof container stored in a cool dry place.

The incredible diversity of the legume family makes it one of the most rewarding families to save seed from.

Cucurbits: cucumbers, melons, pumpkins, summer and winter squash, watermelons

While saving seed from most vegetables and garden fruits (as opposed to tree fruits) is relatively easy, winter squash and melons are probably the easiest. Both winter squash and melons are picked when ripe and have mature seeds inside, ready for the spooning out into a bowl, rinsing, and drying. But while process-

ing the seed is easy, the pollination and cross-pollination is a little complicated. If you want to save pure varieties, you need to isolate species (see below). All cucurbits are outcrossing plants with male and female flowers usually on the same plant. As a

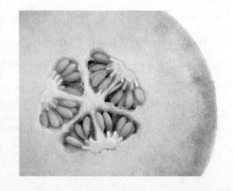

general rule the different species do not cross-pollinate. Varieties in a different genus like watermelons and cucumbers certainly will never cross. So you can grow one variety of each species in your garden with little or no crossing. Since you probably do not want the jack-o'-lantern crossing with the zucchini without your permission, you will need isolation of about one mile, as the bees do the pollination with this one.

1. Melons, watermelons, and winter squash all contain ripe seed when it is eating time, so just cut your squash-o-melon-like fruit it in half and scoop the seeds out into a bowl, avoiding as much pulp as you can.
2. Rinse the seeds off in a strainer, removing the pulp.
3. With a towel, pat them dry; patting through the strainer works well.
4. Leave the seeds out in an airy place until they dry thoroughly.
5. When the seeds are dry, put them in a moisture-proof container, preferably in a cool, dry, place, or in the freezer.
6. Truly dry seeds snap in half when bent, and they do not bend with dampness.
7. Do not forget to label them with the type of seed and date.

Summer squash and cucumbers are different from melons and winter squash because they usually are picked as immature fruit. For seed saving they need to be left to fully ripen, preferably until the plant dies in September/October. Cucumbers will turn into little orange blimps when the seeds are ripe. The summer squash will look like winter squash with the requisite tough, dull skin, and zucchini-shaped squash should be about the size of your leg.

It is also a good idea to let the fruit after-ripen for a week or more after you have picked it before processing for seed. Once fully ripe, seed saving is the same as for melons and winter squash.

The species rundown is:

- Citrullus lunatus (all watermelons and citron melons),
- Cucumis melo (all musk melons, cantaloupes, and honeydews).
- Cucumis sativum (all common cucumbers, except Armenian cucumbers),
- Cucurbita ficifolia (fig-leaved gourd, Malabar gourd)
- Cucurbita maxima (winter squash with corky stems such as buttercup, hubbard, kuri, and sweet meat)
- Cucurbita mixta (winter squash such as: Tennessee sweet potato, cushaws, and Japanese pie)
- Cucurbita moshata (butternuts, cheese, black futsu, and Tromboncino),
- Cucurbita pepo (summer squash such as: zucchini, crookneck, and pattypan; winter squash such as: pie and jack-o'-lantern pumpkins, acorn, delicata, Sugar Loaf, and spaghetti).
- Lagenaria siceraria (bowl/bottle gourds, calabash, or cucuzza)

The different squash species usually do not cross-pollinate. For more information on how to tell them apart and hand pollination techniques, consult *Seed to Seed* by Suzanne Ashworth (more details in the Bibliography section).

If you buy a melon or a winter squash from the store or the farmer's market and save seeds, you probably will get something entirely different from the fruit from whence it came. Most squashes and melons grown today are hybrids, and most are grown in fields with other varieties of the same species, so there is a good chance they are cross-pollinated. Because melon genetics are complicated, you may or may not get something good enough to eat, so save seed at your own risk.

Annual herbs: cilantro, basil, and dill

Biennial herbs: celery, fennel and parsley

Saving seeds from most herbs is easy and beautiful. Cilantro, dill, parsley, and fennel are all in the Apiaceae family. Their flowers form in little umbrella shaped clusters, usually sooner than we, as gardeners, want them to. Saving seed from herbs like cilantro, dill, and fennel has the secondary benefit of providing you with ample seeds for culinary usage. If you want, you can grind the seeds up in a coffee grinder to get a powdery version of the seed. This works really well for cilantro seed (coriander), but maybe not so well for dill.

When you grow **cilantro and dill** in your hydroponic garden, they are somewhat quick to go to seed. All umbels are outcrossers, so you get higher quality seed for the coming years by saving seed from more than one plant. You can start garden plants of each of these herbs from seed purchased in the bulk bins at your local natural food store, or you can buy a specific variety from a seed company.

1. When the center stalk begins to elongate, just let the plants remain where they are growing. They soon will flower and within a month or two, you will have seed dried down and ready to harvest.

2. Once the seed stalk is pretty dry, cut it off at a comfortable length for you to deal with, and put it upside down in a bucket, tote, or paper bag. There may be bugs on it so it might be good to leave it outside (out of the dew) and let the bugs leave. This has the added bonus of letting the seed dry down even more, and it may shatter into the container you have put it in.

3. When the seed is fully dry, thresh by hitting the seed stalk against the sides of the container. You also can break the seeds free with your hands. This has the added bonus of making your hands smell nice, like the herbs.

4. After the seeds are separated from the seed stalk, winnow them free from the rest of the debris by pouring them back and forth between two containers in a breeze or in front of a fan.

Basil is not an umbel and is self-pollinating, but its seeds are processed in the same way as the other annual herbs. Grow three or more plants and rub the seed free from the seed stalk, once the stalk has turned brown. Varieties should be separated by 150 feet. As with most herbs, you can cut some leaves and stems to eat, and you can get a seed crop as well.

Celery, parsley, and fennel are biennials, so they usually flower only after going through the winter months. They need several plants to produce good seed, and the tiny seeds can be saved using the same process as the annual herbs mentioned above.

With all herbs, some seeds are likely to fall off the plant before you process the bulk of the seeds, so you may get some volunteers in the next season if you are lucky.

Lettuce lactuca sativa

The lettuce available for sale in stores or at the farmer's market is an immature plant that has been chopped off right at ground level. So you have to start with lettuce seeds or a young plant start. You probably should start with more than one plant, though, so you can eat a few leaves if that is your inclination.

Lettuce is self-pollinating, so you only need one plant to save seed. All you have to do is put the plant in your hydroponic garden and not eat it, or only eat a few of the outside leaves.

After a month or two (depending on the variety and the weather), the plant will start to bolt. The center of it will elongate, grow to two- to three-feet high, and then begin to flower.

1. Lettuce plants make hundreds of small compound flowers, and each makes a cluster of seeds that look a bit like fingernail clippings or mouse droppings. The seeds often have little duff parachutes on them. The duff resembles a dandelion, as they are in the same family.
2. Pull up the whole plant when most of the seed is ripe.
3. Let the plants sit for a day or two on a tarp (optional). This will cause much of the under-ripe seed to after-ripen.
4. Take a paper bag or a five-gallon bucket and break off the top of the lettuce plant into it.
5. Using a bucket is easy because then you can grab the bottom of the stem (while the plant is upside down in the

bucket, which is right-side up) and whack it against both sides of the bucket. This will shake the seeds out from the plant. Do this until you get all of the seeds off, or as many as you want, and throw the lettuce flower stalk into the compost pile.

6. Alternatively, if you have a lot of plants, you can leave the plants on a tarp and whack the seed heads with a stick. This knocks the seed on the tarp, and you then can remove the seedless plants.

7. Now you should have a good amount of seed, duff, and (maybe) bugs in the bottom of your bucket or tarp.

8. You may want to take a break at this point to let some of the bugs leave and let the seed dry out a little — maybe even overnight, if you have lots of aphids. Lack of critters also makes winnowing easier.

9. Make sure to cover your seed if rain or dew threatens.

10. Take a handful, rub it between your hands to separate the seed from the duff, and continue until most of the seed is separated.

11. Winnow the seeds out from the rest of the debris in the bottom of your bucket. It helps if you have a light breeze, but if not, you can use a fan. If you use a fan, put it on the lowest setting, because lettuce seeds are very light and blow away easily.

12. You will need a second bucket or small container.

13. Pour the seed mixture back and forth between the containers, varying the drop distance depending on the breeze.

14. The mature seeds should drop into the other bucket and everything else should float away. You may need to do this several times before the seed is clean. And if you

have never winnowed anything before, it also might be good to put a tarp on the ground below where you are working so a slight variation in breeze does not blow all of your seeds away, too.

15. Since these seeds are just for you and your friends, they do not have to be super clean — you can stop whenever you have had enough or have enough.

16. Put the seeds on a cookie sheet or a plate so they can finish drying thoroughly, if they are not already.

17. Be sure to mouse-proof their location (either by putting them in a jar or a small hard plastic container), as they are a favorite of mice.

18. If it is stored, very dry lettuce seed will stay viable for five years or more.

Eggplant, tomatillos, and ground cherries

The eggplant that we eat is the unripe fruit. To save seed it is important to forget to pick a fruit or two early in the season and leave it on the plant until it changes color to a dull brownish-purple (for purple eggplants, at least). Others like green or white eggplant turn a kind of dull yellow when ripe. It may be best to wait until the fruit even begins to rot. It is also good to let the fruit

after-ripen for a few weeks before you process the seeds, to make sure the seeds have gotten every speck of goodness from the mother fruit.

Processing of eggplant seed is the same as for tomatillos and ground cherries (a sweet relative of the tomatillos).

1. Cut the fruit in half and scrape out the seeds and pulp.
2. Put the seeds in a bowl or jar, and add water.
3. Stir it up, helping the seed to become free of the pulp by pressing it with your fingers. When you stop stirring, the ripe seeds should sink, and the pulp and immature seeds will float.
4. Carefully pour off (decant) the water, making sure not to go so fast as to pour the seeds that are at the bottom of the jar out with the current.
5. Repeat as many times as you need to, until the seed is clean.
6. If you have a tea strainer, pour the remaining seeds out quickly into the strainer.
7. With a cloth, pat the water out through the bottom of the strainer, and then dump the seeds on a small plate (or yogurt container lid) to dry.
8. Try to keep the seeds only one layer thick to discourage mold.
9. Once the seeds are thoroughly dry, place them in a clearly marked, airtight container.
10. The seeds should last for five years or more.

Peppers: hot and sweet, fresh and dried

Peppers are easy to save seed from. Remember that green peppers and some wax/yellow peppers are not ripe until they turn a different color. The seeds inside are immature. Also, many commercial varieties are F1 hybrids, so the seeds will not grow true-to-type. Be sure to select fruit that is fully ripe, usually red, orange, or yellow, and sometimes purple.

To process the seed of fresh peppers, begin with an exceedingly ripe fruit. No green on the skin.

1. If you have a bell pepper, cut a circle around the calyx and pull out the top. The seed cluster should be attached.
2. Scrape the seeds off the seed cluster, place in a jar with water, mix it up, and proceed as with eggplant seed.
3. The ripe seeds should sink, and the immature seeds and whatever other debris that may have gotten in there will float.
4. Decant and refill the water a few times until the seeds are clean.
5. You can save seeds from dried peppers, but not smoked or roasted ones, more easily than you can from fresh fruit, since the seed is already mostly dry. Germination will be lower because you will not have floated off the hollow seeds.
6. Scrape the seed out, label, dry more if necessary, and store.
7. If the peppers have been dried in a high temperature food dehydrator or in an oven, the seeds may have a lower germination rate or be dead.

8. Remember to wear gloves when working with hot peppers. Cut the fruit in half and scrape out the seeds. If you do not have gloves handy, you can hold the fruit down with a fork and use the tip of a knife or tweezers to scrape the seeds from the fruit so you do not get capsaicin on your fingers.

9. If you must touch spicy peppers with bare hands, be sure to wash your hands thoroughly several times, and do not touch anyone's sensitive parts, like eyes for the rest of the day. Pepper hotness does not wash off easily and can hurt badly.

Spinach and miscellaneous greens

Most modern varieties of spinach were bred by the giant seed-producing companies for spring and summer production or year-round production on the California coast. These commercial hybrids also were developed for freezing and canning industries and a few for the new baby leaf salad market. Locally adapted varieties and winter hardy types have been lost almost completely.

There are some great open-pollinated spinach varieties out there, but most seed catalogues focus their offerings on commercial hybrid varieties that are not suitable for seed saving. The 31 open-pollinated varieties still available (down from 100 in 1981) are disappearing fast, and they need stewards to sweep them up and save them from extinction. Farmers and gardeners who routinely grow spinach could benefit from saving their own seed, as succession sowing consumes a lot of seed.

Spinach (Spinacia oleracea) is relatively easy to save seed from. Most people who have grown spinach in their gardens have had at least a few plants bolt on them. The proper way to save spinach seed is the same process as for any dry-seeded plant, with a few small refinements.

Spinach is an out-breeding, wind-pollinated crop. As such, it needs at least 20 plants (ideally 50 to 100) and isolation from other varieties by one-half to one mile, depending on obstructions and the wind. Spinach is set apart from most other garden plants because it is dioecious: each spinach plant will be male, female, or, rarely, hermaph-roditic. Additionally, in the absence of male plants, some females will "revert" and begin producing male flowers.

Male plants are usually the first to bolt and hold their flowers high above the leaves. They are easy to identify because they shed copious amounts of very fine pollen. Female plants tend to be stockier, and hold their flowers in the leaf axils (where the leaf stem meets the main stem).

Aside from planting out spinach in the spring and waiting, there is a level of sophistication that many spinach seed stewards enjoy. This usually includes over-planting by at least 50 percent and removing the least desirable plants, including many early bolting males. Only a few males are needed to pollinate a female population, so if you rogue out 90 percent of the males, you will allow the females more space, more access to nutrients, and have a higher seed production relative to the total population.

These undesirables may include the quicker bolting male plants (when there are enough male or hermaphroditic individuals remaining), off-types, or individuals with poor hardiness, color, disease resistance, or flavor.

To collect the seeds of spinach and other annual greens such as leaf amaranth, mustard, and collard greens, harvest the plants when the seeds are dry and brown. Threshing by stomping in a tote or on a tarp works well. Be sure to wear shoes when you stomp.

Biennial roots: beets and chard, carrots, turnips, onions, parsnips, leeks

True, onions and leeks are not actually roots, they are a modified leaf. And, of course, chard is not a root at all, but it is the same species as beets. Chard has been selected for a larger leaf instead of a bulbous root. Beets, carrots, parsnips, turnips, and onions are all in different families and have different pollination mechanisms (beets are wind-pollinated, preferring at least two miles isolation, and the others are mostly insect-pollinated and need about one mile). But, their seed is processed in much the same way, so we will just make a seed-saving soup out of them all by putting them in the same pot. Or on the same page, as it were.

All of the plants listed here are biennials. As a rule, biennials are out-crossers and need large populations (30 to 100 plants) for seed saving to avoid inbreeding depression. Also, most of the commercially available carrots and onions (and a good amount of beets) are F1 hybrids, so the seed they produce will not be true-to-type. So, if you want to have good seed, start with seed of high quality open-pollinated varieties to begin with.

For beets and chard, parsnips, carrots, turnips, onions, and leeks for seed production, sow seeds as you
normally would for these
crops, at the same time you
would for an autumn har-
vest. Do not sow carrots for
seed saving in April; wait at

least until June, or they will get too big.

It is a good idea to plant two to three times the amount needed
for a seed crop, so you can have some to eat and cull out the mis-
shapen or off-type ones. Though it may be tempting to eat the
most beautiful beets and carrots, those are precisely the ones you
want to be saving for seed as you steward the variety into its next
generation. So eat your edits.

It is good to dig up all of the crop at once in late fall so you can
look at all the roots (and taste a small piece if you want). From
the hundreds of beets or other biennial roots at your feet, select
the most beautiful and/or vigorous (or whatever you are aiming
for) 50 plants. In the Maritime Pacific Northwest you can replant
right away or in colder climates, return them to earth in early
spring with at least one foot spacing in each direction.

The plants should settle in easily and start to grow shortly after planting. Sit back and watch as they grow more leaves, start
to bolt, and then flower. Biennial root seeds need to be dry processed, so make sure the seeds are completely dry on the plant
before you harvest them. If the seedy part of the plant is dead
brown and almost crispy, the seeds are ready. If the seeds are

mostly dry and a rainstorm is coming, chop off the seed heads and bring them inside to dry down the rest of the way before processing the seed. It is even better to pull up the whole plants and hang them up in the garage to finish drying.

1. Place a tarp under them to catch the shattered seed.
2. Seed processing for biennial roots is similar to that for lettuce.
3. Chop the seed stalks down into a bucket.
4. Leave the plants in buckets or paper bags for a day or two so they can continue to dry down, and the bugs may leave.
5. When you are sure the seed is dry, whack the seed stalk against the sides of your bucket or tote, or dance on top of a pile of seed stalks on a tarp or in a tote.
6. Winnow the seed from the debris using the breeze or a box fan, as you would with lettuce. For parsnips and onions, it is better to hold the seed head and hit it on the inside of a bucket to collect the shattered seed with as little debris as possible, as it is hard to winnow.
7. Let the seeds dry a little more, and when you are sure they are completely dry, label, and store them in a cool, dry place.
8. Please note that the germination rates of onions and parsnips drops severely after the first season, so be sure to share or sow all of your parsnip and onion seeds the spring after you harvest them.

If you are unable to do so, storing in the freezer will preserve them for five years or more.

Brassicas/cole crops: broccoli , collard greens, kale, cabbage, kohlrabi, Brussels sprouts, cauliflower, rutabagas, turnips, radishes, napa cabbage

Brassicas are one of the most important vegetable plant families in our diets today. They are nutritious, delicious, and productive. In the past 100 years, we have lost up to 90 percent of the cabbage and cauliflower varieties in the U.S., as well as huge percentages of other brassicas that were once available through seed companies. This is partly because of the massive consolidation in the seed industry and partly because of the shift within the industry towards F1 hybrids whenever possible. Brassicas are outbreeders and lend themselves easily to being hybridized. This hybridization is good for the seed companies because hybrids produce a uniform crop, perfect for industrial agriculture. Furthermore, the seed from F1 hybrids does not come true-to-type, so if you save seed from a hybrid you may get something very different from what you hoped for. This, in essence, provides a proprietary mechanism for the control of the seed. These factors combine to make brassicas one of the most important threatened food plant families to save seeds from in our gardens. If we do not, the seed companies will not, and then we are in danger of losing very valuable food sources. For seed saving, they are a little more complicated than tomatoes and beans, but the effort is well worth it.

Most of the brassicas we eat in the U.S. are biennials (flowering and producing seed their second year), and most of them are Brassica oleracea. If you leave a broccoli, a collard, a cabbage, a

Brussels sprout, and a cauliflower in your garden, let them flower, and let the bees do their part, you will wind up with hundreds of different brassicas. It is pretty likely none of the next generation will look like what you started with, due to crosses from such diverse parents. Brussels sprouts on a giant kohlrabi base? A collard-leaved cauliflower? A hairy kale?

If you want to save seed from any of these, and you are concerned with getting the seed to produce the same sort of plant you started with, there are three things to know before you start.

1. Most brassicas on the market now are hybrids, and if you save seed from them, you WILL NOT get the same variety.
2. If you are saving a particular variety of Brassica oleracea, you need a large population (50 plants minimum) to maintain a healthy genetic variability. If you want to cross a Brussels sprout with a kale, you can use fewer plants because these two parents are very genetically different from each other.
3. All Brassica oleracea will cross with each other, so you must be sure your neighbors are not letting their collards flower when you are trying to save a purple sprouting broccoli seed crop. Unless, of course, your goal is purple sprouting collards.

For most brassicas, you need to start with seeds or from garden starts. If you sow the seeds in late July and plant the seedlings out by late August, the plants will have sized up enough by fall to hold through the winter and produce flowers the following spring (late April-June). In harsher climates you will have to dig up the plants and store them potted up in a root cellar or greenhouse.

The seed usually dries down by August and forms in dried seed pods all along the branches. If the seed is close to dry and the rains are coming, clip off the plants, and bring them inside.

1. To clean the seeds, just clip off the tops of the plants into a bucket or tote, strip the seed pods from the branches, and dance around in the mess you have made in the bottom of your tote.
2. The dancing should open the seed pods, and the seeds should all fall out.
3. Get another tote or a bucket, and winnow the seed by pouring it from one container to another in a breeze (or in front of a fan), allowing the chaff to float away.

For species isolation please note:

Brassica carinata = Ethiopian/Abyssinian mustard, texsel greens.

Brassica juncea = Indian mustards (like green wave and red giant)

Brassica napus = rutabagas, Russian and Siberian kale.

Brassica oleracea = broccoli, Brussels sprouts, cauliflower, cabbage, collards, kohlrabi, Scotch and Tuscan kale.

Brassica rapa = turnips, broccoli raab and Asian mustards (like pak choi, mizuna, tatsoi and napa cabbage)

Raphanus sativus = radishes (may be biennial or annual)

Crosses between species happen very rarely, but you may flower multiple species at the same time and have isolation.

Cloning

Cloning, in the case of your plants, should not conjure up the white lab-coated scientists working in labs to duplicate sheep. Cloning your plants is simply a matter of taking a cutting from one plant and replanting it to produce another plant that will be of a similar nature to the one you took the cutting from. Follow these instructions, and you should realize a fairly high success rate in your cloning operations:

Tools and equipment:

Small pot for each cutting

Medium for each pot (a loose medium is required such as vermiculite, sphagnum moss, or a combination of loose media)

X-Acto® knife

Nutrient solution

Rooting hormone solution

Procedure:

- Forty-eight hours before cloning, water the plant to be cloned well, and keep it well-watered.
- Place rooting medium (vermiculite, sphagnum moss, etc.) in a small pot.
- Select a healthy plant from which you will take a cutting and water it well.
- Sterilize your X-Acto knife by placing the whole knife or just the blade in boiling water for five minutes.
- Identify a place on the plant to take a cutting. The cutting should be done to a branch where there are two stem

nodules on the section that will be removed, leaving at least two stem nodules on the identified plant.

- To maximize the surface area of the cut, cut the section to be removed from the plant at a 45-degree angle.
- Immediately place the cutting in warm water out of direct sunlight.
- Prepare the pot of rooting medium by poking a small hole in the center.
- Remove the cutting from the warm water, and coat the area of the cut with rooting solution.
- Allow the cutting to rest several days out of direct sunlight.
- Nourish the cutting with watered-down nutrient solution and rooting hormone solution. The solutions should be half-strength compared to what you might normally give your plants.
- Regularly spray the leaves of the cutting with water to keep them from drying out
- In two or three weeks, you should have roots enough on your cutting(s) to place them into your hydroponic system.

Once you have a hydroponic system or multiple systems up and running and you find the types of plants you enjoy growing, you may never have to purchase seeds again if you save seeds and/ or clone your best plants. If you do, indeed, start saving seeds that are healthy and good producers, consider sharing seeds or trading them with friends and family. Encourage them to save seeds, too.

Chapter 10

ONGOING USE AND MAINTENANCE OF YOUR HYDROPONIC GARDEN

*a*s you review the chapters of this book carefully, you will note that one of biggest differences between an outdoor soil-based garden and an indoor hydroponic garden is the level of control the gardener has over the environment and life of the garden. With such a high level of environmental control, you should be able to guard against many of the issues that could cause your plants to suffer. These issues include nutrient deficiencies, pests, and plant diseases.

As you learn and become an experienced hydroponic gardener, your knowledge of the nutrients you feed your plants will grow, and you will grow to understand how, when, and

how much best suits the particular plants you choose in the hydroponic system of your choosing. Chapter 6 has a very comprehensive review of plant nutrients and explains the issues that might arise if your plants get too much or too little of a specific nutrient. If your plants start to develop signs of ill-health and there are not any signs of pests present, review Chapter 6 to determine if your plants are suffering a problem caused by a nutrient deficiency or a nutrient overdose.

Common Pests

If your hydroponic garden is indoors, you will have a great deal of control over pests that can wreak havoc on plants that grow outdoors. By following several simple rules, you should be able to protect your indoor plants from pests.

The best way to protect your plants from pests is to isolate any new plants being brought into your indoor environment for several days before introducing them to your hydroponic system. Plants brought in from the outside or brought in from garden stores can bring in a whole host of pests that will love to feed on your indoor plants. Keeping new plants isolated for several days will allow you to identify any problems before you bring the problems into your clean environment.

The following is a basic list of common garden pests and the signs that your plants may be infested.

Aphids are very tiny white or light-colored insects that will leave a sticky substance on the leaves of your plants. Plants infested with aphids will show curled leaves and weak drooping stems. New growth will be retarded. If you find that your plants are infested with aphids, you should isolate them from the rest of your plants. You can treat plants that have been infested with aphids by rinsing the leaves with warm water and a small amount of dish soap for a week. You also can spray the leaves with an insecticidal soap.

Caterpillars are any worm-like insect and can be seen quite easily. Plants that are infested with caterpillars will have leaves with holes in them (small or large) and/or have torn and/or shredded leaves. Isolate plants that are infested with caterpillars. Thoroughly search the plants and pick off the caterpillars. Keep the plants isolated for several weeks to guard against any new egg hatching.

Cockroaches — These pests are dark brown or black in color and have hard shells. If your plants are infested by cockroaches, it is more than likely that your home or garden place also is infested. Your plants will show signs similar to those signs described above for caterpillars. If you find any cockroaches on your plants, isolate the affected plants, and remove the pests. Place cockroach traps, available in most hardware and/or grocery stores around your garden area and home. You may need to contact an exterminator.

Fungus gnats are small, black flying insects that you will see flying around your plants. While adult fungus gnats are harmless, the maggots hatched will destroy the roots of your plants. Remove and isolate any plants that show signs of fungus gnats. Spray the plant with an insecticidal soap. A plant infested with these pests will wilt considerably, and the leaves will turn yellow. You will notice that the plant roots will appear to be chewed on.

Mealy Bugs are tiny white pests that appear on stem joints. Plants affected with mealy bugs will wilt and lose leaves. Isolate affected plants, and spray with an insecticidal soap. Keep the plant in isolation for at least a week as you inspect it with a magnifying glass for signs of pests.

Spider Mites — These pests cannot be seen by the naked eye. You will see signs of spider mites as rough webs spun under leaves. Also, plants infested by spider mites will develop grey spots. Isolate affected plants. Gently wash the leaves of affected plants with warm water, and spray with an insecticidal soap.

Whiteflies are small white flying insects that you will see flying around your plants. Plants infested with whiteflies will exhibit yellowed leaves that wilt and drop off. A sticky film may appear on leaves. Remove and isolate affected plants, and spray with an insecticidal soap.

If your plants become infested with any of the above pests, or any pests not listed here, you should perform a thorough inspection of all plants in your garden. Some pests, such as cockroaches or whiteflies, are stubborn and hard to eradicate. You may need to treat not only the plants that appear to be infested, but also all of the plants in your garden.

Like so many other issues that may affect the health of your hydroponic garden, prevention is easier than dealing with an infestation of pests. Any plants that you plan to bring in from the outside or that you bring from locations outside of your garden's environment, should be isolated for a week or two as you keep a close eye on them for signs of trouble. Any plants that show signs of pests should be treated or destroyed before you introduce them into your garden.

Common Plant Diseases

As with nutrient imbalance and, in many cases, pest infestation, diseases are most commonly brought about by the gardener's inattentiveness. You will see in the list of common plant diseases that follows that many of the diseases are caused by too much water, too much humidity, inadequate ventilation, and/or a nutrient imbalance. As mentioned earlier, preventive measures usually are easier to carry out than the measures that will need to be taken should your plants develop a disease.

Crown and/or stem rot — Plants will start to show signs of rot as the leaves turn brown and begin to fall off. This will start low on the plant and work its way up. The stem will turn soft and start to rot away. A fungus that grows in medium that is waterlogged and in a hydroponic system that has not been properly cleaned causes this rotting. You are more likely to see this condition in static hydroponic systems. If you determine that your plant(s) are suffering from rot, use a sterile X-Acto knife to cut away the diseased portions of the plant(s). Examine the medium to see if it is waterlogged and stagnant. Allow the medium to dry out and be sure that the system is draining properly.

Mildew — Plants suffering from mildew will appear as if there is mold growing on the leaves, as a grey fuzzy growth will appear. The leaves then will curl up and fall off. Mildew usually is caused by too much humidity and too little ventilation. If you notice that your plants are suffering from mildew, remove the affected parts of the plant, and increase the ventilation of the space in which the garden system is located.

Mold — The hydroponic gardener should watch for several types of mold. Grey mold (which also may appear as a white mold) that grows on leaves is probably caused by waterlogged medium. Remove the affected leaves, and check the drainage of your system. Increasing the ventilation of the space in which the garden system is located may also help. Black mold is the by-product of pests such as aphids. Check your plants for pests, and follow the pest cure and prevention noted in the previous section.

Botrytis — This is a more specific term for a disease that appears on plants as a type of grey mold-like fuzz. This fungus is caused by inadequate ventilation. If you notice that your plants are suffering from this fungus, remove the affected parts of the plant, and increase the ventilation of the space in which the garden system is located.

If you notice that your plants are looking droopy or are stunted, have leaves that are shrivelling and falling off, or they just do not appear healthy, you, more than likely, have plants that are suffering from a nutrient issue, pests, or one of the common diseases noted here. You usually can notice the pest issue easiest. If you see pests, you can act quickly to treat the problem. Nutrient issues and diseases are a little more problematic to identify, but with the notes here, you may be able to do so and treat the malady without too much harm to the affected plant.

As has been mentioned several times already, prevention should be the primary concern of the hydroponic gardener. Because you will control so much of the plant's environment, it is in your power to prevent any of the issues described in this chapter. Keep your environment clean, ventilated, and free of any new plants that may be harboring pests, and you will go a long way toward warding off any potentially damaging issues.

CONCLUSION

The practice of hydroponic gardening is so basic that you well may be able to devise your own system and be successful in growing a wide variety of plants if all you do is read about the overview and history of the practice in the first chapter of this book. Let the water do the work.

Like many other "simple" practices, however, you can dive into the complexities of hydroponic gardening that will allow you to increase productivity and deepen your understanding of plants and their particular needs. Understanding the plant from seed to seed producer is not only fascinating, but it also is essential to the success of your hydroponic garden. Knowing the water and nutrient needs of your plants will help keep your garden flourishing for generations. Knowing the hydroponic system that works best for you and your environment will allow you to best manage your garden in the healthiest way possible. Know your equipment and your system operation. Experiment with and understand how to best control the environment in which your plants will best thrive by learning about light, airflow, and temperature control.

As your plants grow and thrive, keep those desirable plants growing by saving seeds and cloning. Healthy robust plants will beget healthy robust plants.

Dirt-free, low-cost, space-saving, low in pesticides, and environmentally friendly, hydroponic gardening — the art of growing plants without any soil — is a method already used by millions for growing healthy, vibrant plants by everyday gardeners. The results of practiced hydroponic gardening are high-yield production — with a growth rate that is 30 to 50 percent faster than a soil-based plant grown under the same conditions, according to the Pacific Agri-Food Research Centre. You do not have to be a professional horticulturalist to learn how to grow soil-free in your own home. For anyone who was ever turned off by traditional gardening because of inconvenience or messiness, hydroponic gardening offers an attractive and practical alternative.

GLOSSARY

absorb — To take in.

adaptivar — Usually describes a population of an out-crossing species, such as kale or melons, in which many distinct varieties have been allowed to flower together and pollinate each other to create a diverse gene pool. The seeds of an adaptivar produce many unique plants which themselves may or may not produce similar offspring. Essentially, an adaptivar is a collection of many varieties that continually crossbreed with each other.

The population is stewarded by human and/or natural selection to increase the frequency of desirable traits, such as disease resistance or flavor. Also see: grex and landrace.

aerate — To expose to oxygen or air.

agricultural biodiversity — The diversity of crops grown in an agricultural situation. High agricultural biodiversity is achieved when farmers plant multiple varieties of multiple species on their farms, as in a diverse organic vegetable farm.

airstone — A porous stone, the type you find in fish aquariums, which will diffuse the air that is being sent into the reservoir of a hydroponic system by an air pump. Airstone might be a natural material such as limewood or sandstone, but it could also be a man-made commercial product such as a Bubble Wand.

annual — A plant that completes its life cycle and dies in one year, such as lettuce, squash, or tomatoes and peppers. Also see: biennial.

biennial — A plant that requires two growing seasons to complete its life cycle (produce seed and die), such as carrots, beets, onions, or cabbages. These plants all require a vernalization period to trigger bolting. Also see: annual.

biodiversity — The variation of life forms within a given ecosystem or for the entire earth. Biodiversity often is used as a measure of the health of a biological system. Often biodiversity is measured in the number of species present.

bolting — When a plant elongates to begin flowering.

botany — The study of plant life.

brassica — A kind of pet name for any member of the Brassica genus and sometimes members of the wider brassica family (Brassicaceae). A cabbage or mustard relative.

calyx — The ring of leaf-like sepals that surround, protect, and support a flower or fruit.

chaff — The inedible, dry, scaly protective casings of the seeds of cereal grain, or similar fine plant material.

conduct — Transmit energy.

CO_2 — Carbon dioxide, a naturally occurring chemical compound used by plants, along with water, in the process of photosynthesis.

cotyledon — The inner part of a seed that contains stored energy used for growth.

cross-pollinator — A plant that readily shares and accepts pollen with other plants of the same species, sometimes requiring pollen from another plant to set viable seed. This includes corn, carrots, and cabbage among others. Often referred to a "crosser" or "out-breeder." Also see: self-pollinator.

cultivate — To nurture, tend to, and grow a living thing.

dynamic systems — Dynamic systems allow water and nutrients to circulate.

ecotype — A local variant produced through selection pressures of the local ecology. A locally adapted variety is often developed when a seed is saved and stewarded though multiple seasons and is the result of a microevolution that adapts a seed variety to its bioregion or microclimate. Also see: selection, adaptivar, stewardship.

enzyme — Proteins produced in living cells that speed up or increase the rate of a chemical reaction such as the metabolic processes of an organism.

F1 — Refers to the first generation after a cross has been made. See hybrid.

foliar — Of leaves.

fruit — The seed-carrying part of a plant.

genetic diversity — Genetic diversity means that the individuals in a population differ in their inherited attributes. Wild plant populations are typically genetically diverse. A genetically diverse population has the flexibility to adapt.

germ — The embryo of a seed where much of the fats and minerals are stored.

germinate — To start to grow from a seed.

germplasm — A term used to describe the genetic resources for an organism, such as the characteristics of seeds or nursery stock.

grex — An interbreeding population of many distinct varieties. Possibly from the Greek for "herd." Also see: adaptivar and landrace.

heirloom — An open-pollinated variety that has been passed down from generation to generation, though there is disagreement as to how many generations (plant or person) is necessary.

heterosis — Increased vigor of a hybrid when compared to its parental lines. The parental lines are often very inbred, therefore the vigor may not be higher than a similar non-inbred open-pollinated variety.

horizontal resistance — A combination of genes that act together to combat various pathogens or predators, cannot be isolated, and can adapt when those predators adapt, as opposed to Mendelian genetic theory of single gene resistance that can break down rapidly when predators adapt.

horticulture — The science and art of growing and using fruits, vegetables, flowers, ornamental plants, and grasses to improve our environment and to diversify our diets.

humidity — The amount of moisture in the air.

hybrid (F1) — A variety of a plant created by crossing two (usually inbred) parent lines. Due to the genetic trick of heterosis, a hybrid plant is often more uniform and the seed saved from a hybrid (the F2) will segregate and produce plants that do not resemble its parent.

hydroponics — A means of growing plants using water as the singular method of nutrient delivery.

inbreeding depression — A lack of vigor caused by saving seed from too few plants of an outbreeding species.

insect-pollinated — A term used to describe plants such as carrots, broccoli, or onions whose flowers are or can be pollinated by insects.

isolation distance — The distance required between two varieties of the same species in order to save seed that maintains varietal integrity.

landrace — A cultivated plant population that is genetically diverse and genetically flexible. A landrace can respond to selection pressures during cultivation.

Leca — Lightweight expanded clay aggregate.

lumens — Known in other terms as luminous flux, measures the perceived power of light from a natural or artificial light source.

lux — The measurement of the apparent intensity of light at a given distance.

macronutrient — A chemical element, such as nitrogen, phosphorus, potassium, calcium, magnesium, and sulphur, needed in large amounts by plants for growth and development.

micronutrient — A chemical element or compound that living organisms need in small amounts for growth and development.

medium (media) — A substance through which something is carried.

milk stage — The point at which a grain kernel is filed with sugary milky liquid.

mineral — Inorganic matter that must be consumed by plants or animals to remain healthy.

nutrient — Any substance that provides sustenance.

open-pollinated (OP) — A term used to describe a plant whose flowers are fertilized by natural means. A variety that, if properly isolated, will breed true-to-type when saved to plant the following year. An heirloom variety is an example of an OP variety. See also: hybrid.

outbreeder — See cross-pollinator.

perennial — A plant that lives for three or more years and does not die after it sets seed. Fruit trees are an easy example.

perfect flower — A flower that contains both male and female parts: Perfect flowers are bi-sexual.

pH — The pH scale measures how acidic or basic a substance is. It ranges from 0 to 14. A pH of 7 is neutral. A pH less than 7 is acidic, and a pH greater than 7 is basic. Each whole pH value below 7 is ten times more acidic than the next higher value. For example, a pH of 4 is ten times more acidic than a pH of 5 and 100 times (ten times ten) more acidic than a pH of 6. The same holds true for pH values above 7, each of which is ten times more alkaline — another way to say basic — than the next lower whole value. For example, a pH of 10 is ten times more alkaline than a pH of 9. Pure water is neutral, with a pH of 7.0. When chemicals are mixed with water, the mixture can become either acidic or basic. Vinegar and lemon juice are acidic substances, while laundry detergents and ammonia are basic.

photomorphogenesis — The process through which plant growth and development is controlled by light.

photosynthesis — The process employed by green plants to produce simple carbohydrates, using energy that chlorophyll captures.

plant variety protection (PVP) — A form of patent on open-pollinated varieties of plants. If a plant has been registered for PVP protection, it is illegal to save seed to grow out yourself. You must buy seed from a licensee or pay royalties to the license holder. Kamut is a PVP grain.

plumule — The undeveloped primary shoot of a plant embryo.

pollination — The transfer of pollen from a plant's male sex organ to the female sex organ of the same or another plant. Pollination is required to create viable seed.

radicle — A young plant root.

roguing — The negative selection event of removing inferior plants from a population to help improve or maintain a variety. See also: selection.

roots — The lowest portion of a plant that serves to absorb nutrients, aerate the plant, and store nutrients. The roots also serve as a means of anchorage and support.

Seed Saver's Exchange (SSE) — A network of people committed to collecting, conserving, and sharing heirloom seeds and plants. The organization, which was founded in 1975 and is based in Decorah, Iowa, publishes a yearbook wherein members list the seeds they have available to share with other gardeners.

seed swap — A gathering of gardeners and seed savers where seeds are freely exchanged. There are many models for seed swaps, with some (as in the UK, where they are called "Seedy Sundays") charging a small entry fee and a small fee (50 pence) for seeds that are not directly exchanged for other seeds. National Seed Swap Day is January 31.

selection — Choosing the most vigorous or most well-formed plants out of a population for seed-saving purposes. If you eat the plants that are less than optimal, and leave the rest for seed production, you ensure the best genetics for seed. Also see: roguing.

selection event — Conditions that eliminate part of a planting of a specific variety, such as extreme cold, heat, dampness, drought, or pest infestation. For seed-saving purposes, selection events can help a population of plants to evolve under pressure.

self-pollinator — A plant with perfect flowers that usually pollinate themselves and rarely cross with other plants. This includes wheat, beans, tomatoes, and lettuce, among others. Often referred to as a "selfer." (See also: cross pollinator.)

shattering — The breaking open of the seed pod or process by which ripe seeds separate from the seed stalk of a plant when they are dried. Usually, a seed saver wants to harvest and process the seed shortly before this occurs, lest they lose their seed.

shoot — A newly grown part of a plant that has emerged from a seed.

soil — The upper-most layer of most of the earth's surface that is made up of eroded rock and decayed organic matter, as well as bacteria and fungi.

solution — A fluid, or liquid, with two or more substances mixed together and dispersed uniformly throughout.

species — A population of organisms capable of interbreeding in nature. (Interbreeding refers to producing the normal number of fully fertile offspring.)

sprout — To begin to grow from a seed, grain, legume, or nut. The new growth from a seed, grain, legume, or nut.

static system — Static systems do not allow for the circulation of water or nutrients.

stewardship — The mindful care of a place, plant, or anything else. For seed-saving purposes, stewardship is the process by which an open-pollinated variety is maintained or improved through the careful selection of plants from which to save seed.

stock seed — A special selection of seed that is prime quality and has had extra effort selecting it for the traits desired. Usually used by seed companies as the seed sent to the big seed growers to increase to giant quantities for sale. Our stewardship goal, on a non-industrial scale, is to make all the seed we save stock seed quality.

stratification — The process some seeds must go through for successful germination, in which the seed is kept cold and sometimes damp for a period of time before sowing. This may include freezing or refrigeration. The time involved may be a few weeks to a year. Usually, it is for a few months.

thresh — To break seeds free from the plant, seedpods, or hulls.

time isolation — Isolating seed varieties by planting so that pollen is not being shed by different varieties at the same time. This can be done successfully with corn, some mustards, and an annual brassica with a biennial variety of the same species.

variety — A type of plant, for example a tomato, which can be distinguished from other types of the same species. A yellow Galina cherry tomato is a different variety than a red Peacevine cherry tomato.

vegetable — Any part of a plant you eat that is not the fruit or seed.

vegetative — The growth stage of a plant that is typically characterized by leaf and stem growth. The other stages of plant growth that are not considered vegetative are flowering and fruiting. However, there is typically some vegetative growth during flowering and fruiting stages.

vernalization — A period of cold (the winter months) that a biennial must go through before it is triggered to produce flowers (and then seeds). Also, some seeds must go through a vernalization process (known as stratification) before they can germinate.

volunteer — A plant that grows without having been deliberately planted.

wind-pollinated — A term used to describe plants whose pollen is distributed through the wind. This includes beets chard, corn, spinach, and rye grain.

winnow — To separate the seed from the chaff, usually using wind or a fan.

RESOURCES

Seeds

Burpee is, perhaps, America's most recognized seed retailer. **www.burpee.com**

High Mowing Organic Seeds offers organically grown seeds to gardeners and farmers. **www.highmowingseeds.com**

Johnny's Selected Seeds is an online retailer of seeds and garden tools. **www.johnnyseeds.com**

Ornamental Edibles is an international mail-order seed business serving home gardeners, specialty markets growers, and hydroponic growers. **www.ornamentaledibles.com**

Richters is an online retailer located in Canada that deals primarily in herbs. **www.richters.com**

Seeds of Change® offers organically grown seeds to gardeners and farmers. **www.seedsofchange.com**

Stokes Seeds is a distributor of flower, vegetable, and herb seeds as well as many garden accessories. www.stokeseeds.com

Supplies

Hydroponics Simplified is an online hydroponics supplier featuring wide selection of hydroponic systems and supplies for hobby and commercial growers. www.hydroponics-simplified.com

Illumitex® offers the world's most advanced LED lighting for growers. www.illumitex.com/led-lights-for-indoor-gardening

Stealth Hydroponics is an online hydroponics supplier featuring wide selection of hydroponic systems and supplies for hobby growers. www.stealthhydroponics.com

BIBLIOGRAPHY

Kleeger, Sarah and Still, Andrew. *A Guide to Seed Saving, Seed Stewardship & Seed Sovereignty*. Sweet Home, Oregon, 2010.

Nicholls, Richard E. *Beginning Hydroponics, Soil-less Gardening, The Beginner's Guide to Growing Vegetables, Houseplants, Flowers, and Herbs without Soil*. Philadelphia: Running Press, 1977.

Resh, Howard M. *Hobby Hydroponics*. Boca Raton, Florida: CRC Press, 2003.

Roberto, Keith. *How-To Hydroponics*. Massapequa, New York: Electron Alchemy, Inc., 1994.

Stash, Grubbycup. *Grubbycup's Garden Notes*. Denver, Colorado: Chlorophyll-NCWGS, 2011.

Van Patten, George F. *Gardening Indoors with Soil & Hydroponics*. George F. Patton, 2008.

Van Patten, George F. *Hydroponic Basics*. George F. Patton, 2004.

AUTHOR BIOGRAPHY

Rick Helweg has written numerous books on food, gardening, communications, and not-for-profit issues for Atlantic Publishing Group. He is an award-winning baker and writer! Rick is also the director of Research and Communications for Teach a Kid to Fish, a children's health initiative whose mission is to prevent and reduce childhood obesity by empowering Lincoln children and families to eat healthy and be active. Rick, his family, and garden lives in Lincoln, Nebraska.

INDEX